Advanced Genealogy
Research Techniques

About the Authors

George G. Morgan (left) and Drew Smith (right)

George G. Morgan has been the president of Aha! Seminars, Inc. since 1996. He is an internationally recognized genealogy expert who presents at local, state, national, and international genealogical conferences. He also presents genealogy webinars and speaks on genealogy cruises.

He is the prolific author of hundreds of genealogy articles for magazines, journals, newsletters, and websites in the United States, Canada, the United Kingdom, and Singapore. He is the author of three editions of *How to Do Everything: Genealogy*. This is his eleventh book.

George is Vice President of Membership for the Federation of Genealogical Societies (FGS), and a past President of the International Society of Family History Writers and Editors (ISFHWE). He is a past director of the Florida State Genealogical Society and of the Florida Genealogical Society of Tampa. He is a member of the Association of Professional Genealogists (APG), the International Society of British Genealogy and Family History (ISBGFH), and a number of genealogical societies.

Drew Smith, MLS, has been a librarian at the University of South Florida (USF) Tampa Library since 2007, and was previously an instructor for the USF School of Library and Information Science (now the School of Information). He is a respected and popular speaker at local, state, and national conferences. He has written numerous articles for genealogical magazines, and is currently the "Rootsmithing with Technology" columnist for the Federation of Genealogical Societies' *FORUM* magazine. Drew is the author of the book *Social Networking for Genealogists*, published in 2009 by Genealogical Publishing Company. In 2013, he was selected to serve as the first Chair of the Family History Information Standards Organisation (FHISO). Since 2007, Drew has been the President of the Florida Genealogical Society of Tampa. He is a Director of the Federation of Genealogical Societies, Chair of the FGS Technology Committee, and a past Secretary of the Association of Professional Genealogists (APG).

George and Drew together produce The Genealogy Guys[SM] Podcast, the longest running genealogical podcast, published online at genealogyguys.com and enjoyed by thousands of listeners around the world.

Advanced Genealogy Research Techniques

George G. Morgan
Drew Smith

New York   Chicago   San Francisco   Athens
London   Madrid   Mexico City   Milan
New Delhi   Singapore   Sydney   Toronto

Cataloging-in-Publication Data is on file with the Library of Congress

Advanced Genealogy Research Techniques

234567890   DOC DOC   109876543

ISBN   978-0-07-181650-2
MHID   0-07-181650-X

Sponsoring Editor	Roger Stewart
Editorial Supervisor	Patty Mon
Project Manager	Harleen Chopra, Cenveo® Publisher Services
Acquisitions Coordinator	Amanda Russell
Copy Editor	Nancy Rapoport
Proofreader	Vicki Wong
Indexer	Ted Laux
Production Supervisor	Jean Bodeaux
Composition	Cenveo Publisher Services
Illustration	Cenveo Publisher Services
Art Director, Cover	Jeff Weeks
Cover Designer	Jeff Weeks

We dedicate this book with love and gratitude to all of our genealogy friends, from whom we have learned and with whom we have shared over the years. You make our journey very special.

Contents

Acknowledgments

The creation of any book is always a collaborative effort that involves the knowledge, talents, and skills of many individuals. We would like to mention a few of the people who have helped us realize our vision for this book.

We want to extend our sincere thanks to members of the McGraw-Hill Education team. We are grateful to Roger Stewart, Editorial Director at McGraw-Hill Education, for his strong commitment and support for this book. We'd like to thank Amanda Russell, our Editorial Coordinator, for her excellent guidance and assistance throughout our production of each part of the book. A big thank you also goes to Megg Morin, editor of George's *How to Do Everything: Genealogy* books, who facilitated the beginning of this book's production. The McGraw-Hill Education team members are always highly professional, and we're very appreciative of the friendships we have formed with all the members of the team.

George would also like to thank the many readers of *How to Do Everything: Genealogy* who have asked, "When is the next book coming out?" and "How do I get past this brick wall?" The authors have long known that a more advanced book was needed, and the readers have provided the impetus to produce this volume.

We'd also like to thank our genealogy friends, colleagues, and podcast listeners. They have shared their experiences, proposed research strategies and solutions to difficult problems, and offered us their friendship and support. We all learn from one another, and we enjoy passing the knowledge forward.

Introduction

When the Going Gets Tough...

The quest for information about our ancestors and their families can be exciting and fulfilling. The thrill of the chase provides countless opportunities to learn about the places they lived, the historical period in which they lived, the events that influenced them or in which they participated, and the other people in their lives. It is gratifying to place these people into context and to come to *really* know and understand them.

The hobby of genealogy is different from most other hobbies in that it often starts out very easy and then gets more difficult the more you work with it. Unless you're dealing with a comparatively recent adoption situation or a parent or grandparent who was reluctant to talk about their families, you can often begin your research and make quick progress in filling out the names of your parents, grandparents, and possibly even your great-grandparents. However, once you get past the information that the family already knows, and have exhausted information found in the documents you find in your own home or in the possession of close relatives, you will discover that you have to learn about how to locate and use records of genealogical interest, such as obituaries, census records, and vital records. You may again make significant progress and work back in time at least into the nineteenth century, although your success may be frustrated by dealing with ancestors who came from other countries and whose points of origin may be unknown. Your work may be stymied by places where the records aren't easily accessible or that are in a language that you don't speak.

At each generation, you're doubling the number of trails to follow, and some are going to be much easier than others. A few of these trails may connect to published genealogies that already provide excellent reference sources that lead to strong documentation. Most, however, are going to be untraveled territory. Sooner or later, you're going to be following that path through the dark forest of time, and come upon the dreaded brick wall. Your basic knowledge of genealogical research may prove insufficient to get past that wall, and you may become frustrated and discouraged.

This book is intended to help.

...the Tough Get Going

George's previous book, *How to Do Everything: Genealogy,* is written with the beginning genealogist in mind. It provides a basic set of research skills and identifies many of the common types of records available to researchers.

This book is not for beginners, but for those who have already mastered the level of content found in *How to Do Everything: Genealogy,* and who have now run up against brick walls and need some additional skills to make further progress. This means that we will assume that you already know about the various genealogical record types and where to find them, and that you already know the essential processes involved in searching for information both online and offline. We also presume that you have experience researching online using both Internet search engines and genealogy database sites, and that you already know the standard ways of entering, manipulating, and reporting genealogical information, especially using genealogy software.

So this book is going to take you to the next level by presenting you with a set of techniques that can help you make progress when the beginning methods aren't enough. It will also help you better comprehend and understand the content of some of the common genealogical evidence that you *thought* you knew.

The Brick Wall Metaphor (and Why It Matters)

The best way to learn something new is to relate it to something that you already understand or can easily visualize. This is why good educators, whether standing up in front of a classroom, leading a webinar, or writing a textbook, try to think about where their students are in the learning process and what they already are likely to know. We learn this way because our brains can quickly make new connections when they are linked to existing knowledge.

When we decided to write this type of book, we realized that our readers would need an easy way to remember these new techniques, a way to relate them to something that they could easily imagine. And if the problem faced by a genealogist is called a "brick wall," then why not use the mental image of a brick wall as a way to explain how each of these research techniques works? Analogies are great "connectors" and we'll use them to help you extend your knowledge.

So now, in your mind's eye, imagine yourself standing in front of a dense forest. There is one entrance into the forest that is the beginning of a path, and your passage along that path is your genealogical research journey. The beginning of the path is analogous to yourself, and the path is easy to walk along because you already know an awful lot about yourself (whether from personal memory, the memories of others, or from documents you possess). What happens, however, when the path forks?

You can take the left fork (your father's side of the family), or the right fork (your mother's side). Again, unless you have already reached an adoption situation or you have a secretive or absent parent, either fork provides a distinct path that you can choose to move along. No matter which path at the fork you take, you can always return to the fork later and try the other path, too. As long as there are relatives alive to provide dependable information or documents to be found using basic genealogical research techniques, you can make good time as you walk along the path and make choices at each fork (as you move from generation to generation).

What happens when the path reaches a brick wall? It may be a high wall, so high that you can't see over it, and it stretches across the entire path so that you can't simply walk around it (at least not that you can see). Your progress along the research path has stopped. What choices do you have to help you make further progress? That depends a great deal on the approach you take from there.

Eight Ideas for Getting Past the Brick Wall

There are numerous approaches you can take, depending on what you want to learn and the place and time in which your ancestor lived.

- You can get up very close to the wall and examine the entire wall in detail, checking to see if there are any weaknesses you can push through.

- You can go back home, and return with a sledgehammer, and keep striking the wall as hard as you can until it gives way. That might take a while.

- You can examine the ends of the wall, and see if there's a way to travel around it.

- You can return home and describe your brick wall to each person that you encounter. Maybe someone else has an idea for getting past that particular brick wall.

- You can get a large number of people to help you all at the same time. They can form a human pyramid that you can climb and that might help you over the wall.

- You can return home and bring back a ladder.

- You can hire a demolition expert who has years of experiencing in breaking through brick walls.

- You can give up, for now, and follow one of the other paths, and return to this brick wall later. Maybe it will have crumbled a bit or you'll have some additional ideas on how to get past it.

Could you visualize each of those solutions as a way to get past a brick wall? If so, you're ready to see how we turn the brick wall metaphor into realistic ways to attack and help solve your genealogical research brick wall problems.

Keep in mind that just one research technique may help you work past a brick wall and locate the evidence you seek. However, you may use a first research technique to seek out evidence for one type of fact and a second technique for another, related fact. You may actually employ *multiple techniques* in a particular sequence, or you may alternate back and forth as you gather and build a collection of evidence.

We collect genealogical information in many formats from many different places. Humans love to talk and write about themselves, and governments have long sought to document their citizens for a wide variety of reasons. The evidence that genealogists use includes original documents, books, letters, newspapers and periodicals, online databases and websites, verbal conversations, and many other sources. We search for these materials in many places. Unfortunately, we rarely obtain the evidence we seek in the chronological sequence as our ancestors lived their lives. We locate one piece of information here, another there, and yet another one somewhere else.

We also know that not all evidence is created equal. Some pieces of evidence are stronger and more accurate than others. Some items are primary sources of information while others are secondary. Some materials are original documents while others may have been derived from other materials. It is therefore essential to *cite and study* our sources so that we can effectively evaluate and weigh the evidence as we conduct our research.

Despite the attention we pay to the details, it is inevitable that we will encounter brick walls. These impasses can be extraordinarily frustrating, but they are not always impossible to get past.

What You'll Need Before You Set Out

No matter which technique you are learning to use, there are some basic preparations that you'll need to make before starting. Regardless of whether your genealogical research is basic or advanced, you first need to:

1. Identify your research goals and objectives. They can help ensure that you conduct a more thorough investigation and locate as many needed records as you want. Whenever planning any research, it is important to identify the person(s) whose information you are seeking and to define the question(s) you hope to answer. It is essential to consider the time period in which the person lived, the geographical location, the government and other record-generating entities in operation there and then, and what documents might have been created to record the fact(s) that you are seeking. Ask yourself, when you reach a logical stopping point in your research, what is it that you hope to have accomplished? Are you trying to identify an immigrant ancestor? Join a lineage society? Find all of the descendants of an ancestor in preparation for a family reunion? Or just take each of your lines as far back in time as you can until original documentary evidence runs out?

2. Identify your research questions. Do you want to know the maiden name of a female ancestor? Are you trying to determine the ancestral hometown of an immigrant? Do you want to learn more about the military service of an ancestor and where that service may have taken him? The more specific your questions are, the easier it will be to stay focused and on track. Write them down and describe specifically what you want to answer.

3. Identify the resources that are most likely to be relevant to the place and time of the events involved with your research question. Don't limit yourself to only online databases and webpages. Be sure to include a combination of both printed *and* electronic resources.

4. For each goal and research question, consider what records were created at the location and the time your ancestor lived there. Consider the types of information that those records may have contained. Determine whether those records still exist and where they are now located. If the records no longer exist or can't be located, what other alternative source(s) may provide the same or similar details? Finally, you will need to discover where and how you can access those records.

If you have all of these things defined and clear in your mind, set them down on paper as your research roadmap. You are then ready to start your journey through that dense, sometimes dark, forest of history, and we'll show you in the next nine chapters what to do when that brick wall appears.

Not only will we describe each technique in detail, including some of the more common variations, but also we'll frequently provide case study examples that illustrate how the technique can be used in actual practice to break past brick walls. We'll also include images of documents and computer screenshots to illustrate the tools and techniques we use. We encourage you to retrace our research steps so that you gain first-hand, in-depth experience. We'll also relate stories of how we and other researchers have worked to solve brick walls. In the process, we hope that you will gain new insights and come up with new ideas to help you get past some of your own genealogical brick walls.

1

Examine the Brick Wall in Detail

Most of us have heard the expression, "The devil is in the details," meaning that details are extremely important and that ignoring the details can result in serious problems later on. One popular example of this is commonly found in mystery fiction, such as novels and TV shows. We love the character of Sherlock Holmes because he notices details that others miss and, by noticing those details, he solves the mystery. On many modern TV crime dramas, the forensic scientists painstakingly examine the crime scene, collecting trace evidence that ultimately leads to information about how the victim died, where they died, and who committed the criminal act.

In some cases, the crime scene investigators and police detectives realize that they may have missed something important, and they go back to take another look at evidence that they had already reviewed. Not only does this bring to light things that were originally overlooked, but it also provides an opportunity to see the evidence in a new way because the investigator may have learned something since the last time the evidence was examined that will turn seemingly irrelevant or unimportant information into something relevant and important.

To return to our original brick wall metaphor, a close examination of the wall may discover a weak spot that can be exploited into a breakthrough. Clearly, this may take some time, hard work, and patience. Imagine taking a close look at every brick in that wall, seeing if it can be wiggled or removed. This is painstaking, exhausting work, but it may be all that stands between failure and success.

Now that you have that image in your mind of examining the entire brick wall in detail (perhaps using a flashlight and a magnifying glass) or, if you prefer, an image of yourself as a crime scene investigator, working to collect every tiny trace of evidence for processing in your crime lab, we can turn our attention to how this concept works in the real world of genealogical research.

Reexamine in Detail the Evidence You Have Already Discovered

When you are dealing with a genealogical brick wall, you have probably acquired a number of diverse materials already. These probably include numerous personal papers, family photographs, census records, vital records, newspaper clippings, and other information linked to the individual who is the subject of your brick wall. There may be other materials, including original documents or microfilmed or digitized images of them, that you may not have found or accessed yet. These pieces of evidence may lead to a breakthrough in your brick wall, but you will still need to search for, locate, and obtain copies of them.

If you have not already done so, this may be a good time for you to digitize any relevant paper documents. This will enable you to quickly magnify the document on your computer screen, making some details easier to read and interpret, especially if they are photographs or if they contain handwritten information. (This will also make it easier for you to use some of the other techniques outlined in this book, such as those described in Chapters 4, 5, and 7.)

You may also find it useful to have either one very large computer display screen or multiple computer monitors, enabling you either to put two documents side by side or to put a document alongside a list, report, or chart from your genealogy database software. We'll talk more about genealogy software in a moment. Side-by-side examinations allow you to do such things as compare one photograph with another, compare a household in one census with the same household in a later census, or compare one signature with another. This type of comparison often may cause an unusual detail to jump out at you that you had not noticed before.

When looking at a document that you have seen before, it is tempting to be skeptical that anything new will result from another look. After all, you may have looked at that document several times before, perhaps dozens of times. Would yet another look reveal anything new? Because this kind of work can be mentally exhausting, it is easy to give up too quickly, and in so doing, miss that critical clue that was staring you in the face the entire time. Often, too, when you reexamine a document, some piece of previously meaningless information may now yield an important new clue.

Before we get to specific cases, let's discuss some general ideas of what you are looking for.

Focus on Details You May Have Missed or Overlooked the First Time

For each type of common genealogical document discussed here, we'll start with what you likely noticed first, and then what details you may have failed to take note of. (Note that not every possible detail mentioned would appear in each type of record, as records vary depending upon the geographic location and the time period in which they are produced. The details listed are not intended to be an exhaustive list.)

Census

What you originally noticed:

- The year the census was taken
- The general geographic area (U.S. state/county, Canadian province/district, or British county/civil parish)
- The names of primary members of the household (parents, children) and their ages as they appear in the index

What you may have overlooked:

- The official enumeration date for that year's census
- The actual enumeration date listed at the top of the census form
- The details of the place being enumerated (such as a U.S. incorporated/unincorporated place, ward, township, institution, and enumeration district; a Canadian sub-district; or a British town, ecclesiastical parish, or registration district)

■ The street address of the household

■ Whether the residence was owned or rented

■ The value of property

■ The names of primary members of the household and their ages as they appear on the actual census image

■ The sex, race, marital status, total number of children, number of living children, place of birth, places of their parents' births, occupation (or if they were a student), place they worked

■ Who else lived in the household other than the heads of the household and their children (parents of the head of household, siblings, aunts and uncles, in-laws, boarders)

■ Whether or not they were literate, and what language they spoke

■ Who lived in nearby households (we'll come back to this detail in Chapter 3)

■ Other notations made by the census enumerator (perhaps above, below, or in the margins)

■ Other non-population schedules you may not have investigated for the household

Birth Certificate/Index

What you originally noticed (see Figure 1-1):

■ The general geographic area or jurisdiction for the place of birth

■ The name of the child

■ The date of birth

What you may have overlooked:

■ The details of the place of birth (such as a town, a street address, or a particular hospital)

■ The time of birth

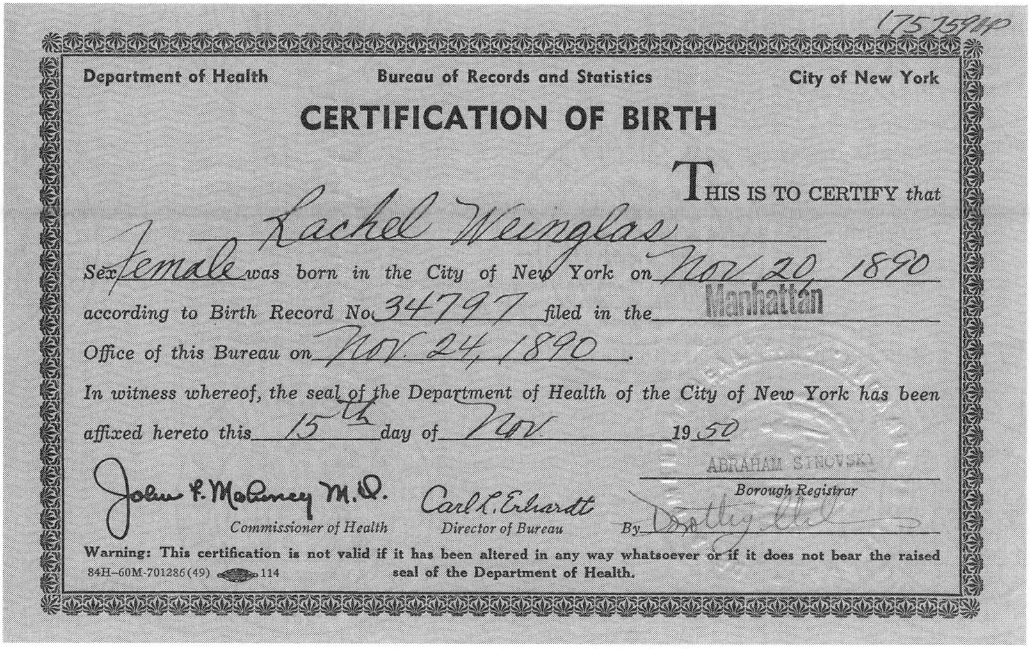

FIGURE 1-1 Birth certificate for Rachel Weinglas[s]. Note that this is a 1950 extraction of information for an 1890 birth.

- Whether the child was born alive or dead
- The sex and race of the child
- The name of an attending physician/midwife or of an informant
- The names of the parents
- The residence of the parents
- The occupation of the father
- The birthplaces of the parents
- Other typed or handwritten notations (such as whether the child was a twin)

Marriage License/Index

What you originally noticed:

- The general geographic area or jurisdiction for the place of marriage
- The names of the marriage partners
- The date of the marriage

What you may have overlooked:

- The ages of the marriage partners
- The birth dates and locations of the marriage partners
- The date of the application for the license
- The date the license was issued
- The name and occupation of the person who performed the ceremony
- The names of the witnesses
- The date the license was returned
- The signatures of the marriage partners
- The names of others who were married on the same date at the same location (in other words, possible double marriages)

Death Certificate/Index

What you originally noticed (see Figure 1-2):

- The general geographic area or jurisdiction for the place of death
- The name of the deceased
- The date of death

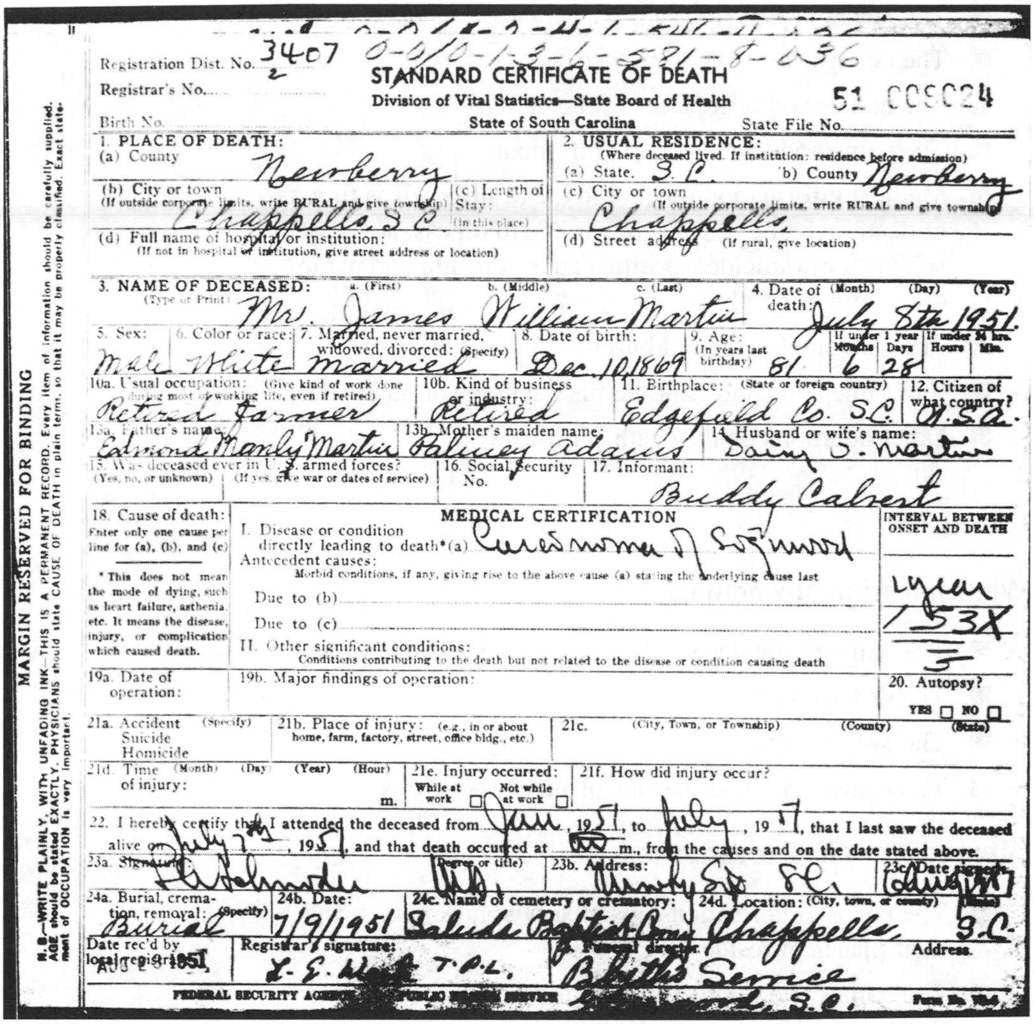

Registration Dist. No. 3407 2 0-0/0-1-3-6-581-8-036
Registrar's No.

STANDARD CERTIFICATE OF DEATH
Division of Vital Statistics—State Board of Health
State of South Carolina

51 008024

Birth No. State File No.

1. PLACE OF DEATH: (a) County Newberry
(b) City or town (If outside corporate limits, write RURAL and give township) Chappells, S.C. (c) Length of Stay: (in this place)
(d) Full name of hospital or institution: (If not in hospital or institution, give street address or location)

2. USUAL RESIDENCE: (Where deceased lived. If institution: residence before admission)
(a) State S.C. (b) County Newberry
(c) City or town (If outside corporate limits, write RURAL and give township) Chappells
(d) Street address (If rural, give location)

3. NAME OF DECEASED: (Type or Print) a. (First) b. (Middle) c. (Last) Mr. James William Martin
4. Date of death: (Month) (Day) (Year) July 8th 1951

5. Sex: Male 6. Color or race: White 7. Married, never married, widowed, divorced: (Specify) married 8. Date of birth: Dec. 10 1869 9. Age: (In years last birthday) 81 If under 1 year Months 6 Days 28 If under 24 hrs. Hours Min.

10a. Usual occupation: (Give kind of work done during most of working life, even if retired) Retired farmer 10b. Kind of business or industry: Retired 11. Birthplace: (State or foreign country) Edgefield Co. S.C. 12. Citizen of what country? U.S.A.

13a. Father's name: Edmond Manly Martin 13b. Mother's maiden name: Paliney Adams 14. Husband or wife's name: Daisy O. Martin

15. Was deceased ever in U.S. armed forces? (Yes, no, or unknown) (If yes, give war or dates of service) 16. Social Security No. 17. Informant: Buddy Calvert

18. Cause of death: Enter only one cause per line for (a), (b), and (c) *This does not mean the mode of dying, such as heart failure, asthenia, etc. It means the disease, injury, or complication which caused death.

MEDICAL CERTIFICATION
I. Disease or condition directly leading to death*(a)
Antecedent causes: Morbid conditions, if any, giving rise to the above cause (a) stating the underlying cause last
Due to (b)
Due to (c)
II. Other significant conditions: Conditions contributing to the death but not related to the disease or condition causing death

INTERVAL BETWEEN ONSET AND DEATH: 1 year

19a. Date of operation: 19b. Major findings of operation: 20. Autopsy? YES ☐ NO ☐

21a. Accident (Specify) Suicide Homicide 21b. Place of injury: (e.g., in or about home, farm, factory, street, office bldg., etc.) 21c. (City, Town, or Township) (County) (State)

21d. Time (Month) (Day) (Year) (Hour) of injury: m. 21e. Injury occurred: While at work ☐ Not while at work ☐ 21f. How did injury occur?

22. I hereby certify that I attended the deceased from Jan 19 51, to July 19 51, that I last saw the deceased alive on July 7th, 1951, and that death occurred at m., from the causes and on the date stated above.

23a. Signature: 23b. Address: 23c. Date signed:

24a. Burial, cremation, removal: (Specify) Burial 24b. Date: 7/9/1951 24c. Name of cemetery or crematory: Salude Baptist Church 24d. Location: (City, town, or county) (State) Chappells, S.C.

Date rec'd by local registrar: AUG 2 3 1951 Registrar's signature: Funeral director: Blythe Service Address: S.C.

FEDERAL SECURITY AGENCY PUBLIC HEALTH SERVICE

N.B.—WRITE PLAINLY, WITH UNFADING INK—THIS IS A PERMANENT RECORD. Every item of information should be carefully supplied. AGE should be stated EXACTLY. PHYSICIANS should state CAUSE OF DEATH in plain terms, so that it may be properly classified. Exact statement of OCCUPATION is very important.

MARGIN RESERVED FOR BINDING

FIGURE 1-2 Death certificate for James William Martin

What you may have overlooked:

- The details of the place of death
- The sex, race, and marital status of the deceased
- The name of the spouse
- The date and location of birth

- The age at death
- The occupation of the deceased
- The names and birthplaces of the parents
- The name and address of the informant
- Medical information relating to the death, such as time of death; whether the death was due to illness, accident, suicide, or homicide; specific cause of death; and name of the attending physician
- The date and location of burial
- The name and address of the funeral home or undertaker
- Other notations on the death certificate

Obituary

What you originally noticed:

- The name of the deceased
- The date of death
- The age at death
- The names and relationships of survivors

What you may have overlooked:

- The names and relationships of survivors, spouses, and their places of residence
- The names and relationships of those who pre-deceased the deceased
- The cause(s) of death
- The names of pallbearers (both actual and honorary)
- Biographical details about the deceased (birth date and location, ethnic background, places lived and migration activity, occupations, education, religious affiliation, military service, organizational memberships, hobbies, awards)
- The location of the funeral service (religious facility, funeral home, or other place)

- The name of the person performing the funeral service and their religious affiliation
- The name and address of the funeral home
- The date and location of burial
- Memorial information

Tombstone/Cemetery

What you originally noticed:

- Name on the tombstone
- Dates of birth and death (or age at death)
- Relationship (husband, wife, father, mother, and so on)

What you may have overlooked:

- Style of the tombstone
- Quality of the tombstone (suggesting its cost)
- Age of the tombstone (original to year of death, or a later addition or replacement)
- Any indication of the producer of the tombstone
- Symbolism used on the tombstone, such as that indicating religious or organizational affiliation, or military service
- Epitaphs
- Significance of multiple names on the same tombstone
- How multiple tombstones are positioned in relation to each other

Photograph

What you originally noticed (see Figure 1-3):

- People of primary interest
- Names, dates, and locations written on the photograph

FIGURE 1-3 Photograph of Virginia and Corinne Martin

What you may have overlooked:

- The name of the photographic studio
- Style of clothing
- Style of hair or facial hair
- How people are arranged in relationship to one another
- Whether or not people resemble one another
- Signs, structures, and landmarks in outdoor scenes
- Other things in the photograph (pets, furniture, jewelry, automobiles, other accessories, and so on)

Now That You Have More Details...

Clearly, we could continue to identify other types of documents, such as military records, immigration and naturalization records, city directories, maps, land and property records, wills and probate records, religious records, and all of the other common record types, and go through the same process of listing the things you'd likely notice first and the details you might have missed, but the examples already provided should give you the guidance you need to think about more details you should examine for any kind of genealogical record. Not only should all of this tell you that you should be looking at new documents carefully, but also that you should return to the same documents again and again, reexamining them for details that you may have missed the first time. We urge you to *reread documents* every time you look at them as if you have never seen them before. You may have learned new information since you last looked at a particular document, and now the seemingly unimportant scrap of information may take on greater significance.

Some of these details will point you to techniques that we will cover in later chapters. For instance, a puzzling detail in an index or abstract may lead you to seek out the original document (we cover this in Chapter 2). An unfamiliar name in a record may cause you to do some research to determine exactly who that person is (see Chapter 3). An unfamiliar place, term, or abbreviation may suggest that you should ask friends or people online to give their opinions (see Chapters 4 and 5).

Organize What You Have in a Genealogy Database Program

When you began your genealogical research process, you likely downloaded and installed genealogy database software in order to keep track of what you had discovered. It's simply not possible for you to remember everything that you find, and paper-based systems are difficult to search or to share with others.

So let's assume that you are using a typical genealogy software program that allows you to enter factual information found in the records you've discovered. You've entered personal names, dates, and places, and you have used standard citation templates so that you know exactly what type of evidence you used, where each item of information came from, and the quality of that source. Is that enough? No. Let's look at how you can use your genealogy software to keep track of details.

Names

What you probably entered:

- Given names (first and middle)
- Surnames
- Suffixes such as "Jr." or III

What you may have forgotten to enter:

- Prefixes (military, religious, or professional)
- Nicknames
- Alternate names (variant spellings, initialisms, aliases, translations)
- Notes about the name (where the name came from, such as a namesake; time frames during which a particular form or spelling of the name was used; specific documents in which the name was found)
- Your thoughts about why the name may have appeared in documents in an inconsistent manner (these can also be entered in the Notes area)

Dates

What you probably entered:

- As much as you knew of the year, month, and day, whether exact or an approximation

What you may have forgotten to enter:

- Alternative dates where the documents are vague or disagree with each other
- Notes about the date (whether the document provided an explicit date or whether the date was calculated from an age, such as found on a tombstone)
- Your thoughts about your confidence in the date and your process for coming up with a reasonable explanation for any date conflicts among documents (such as transcription errors, unreliable witnesses, or intentional misrepresentation)

Places

What you probably entered:

- The name of the place, together with the general geographic area in which it is found

What you may have forgotten to enter:

- The correct geopolitical area (county, province, parish, shire, district, or other designation) in which the place was located *at the time of the event*
- Notes about the place (the actual spelling as it appears in the document, alternate spellings, and other place details)

Create an Ancestor Timeline

Every piece of evidence you collect can provide you with some rather obvious information. Sometimes, however, these materials can supply additional important clues or suggest other details that can help you advance your research.

You will obtain information and acquire evidence in many formats and from many disparate sources over time. These materials are pieces of a much larger puzzle. Since these things come to you in no particular sequence over time, it is important to periodically reexamine them as a body of evidence, just as crime scene technicians do.

George strongly recommends the production of an ancestral profile, or timeline, using all of the evidence you have acquired over time. A number of steps are involved but the process inevitably clarifies the status of your research on an individual (or family group). It also focuses your attention on the quality of each informational source, conflicting information, and gaps in your knowledge of the person.

Some genealogy database programs can produce the type of ancestor timeline described in the following sections. However, to do so you must enter each piece of evidence and each event as a documented "fact" rather than as a text note. In order to produce the most detailed and accurate ancestor profile or timeline, follow the steps in the sections that follow.

Gather All of the Evidence You Have Collected

Locate every piece of evidence that you have acquired over time. If you have transcribed records that now are available as digitized images at online sites, such as census schedules, ships' passenger lists, military pension files, indexes, and other materials, take the time to now go back and obtain images of the original records. If some of this information has not yet been digitized, such as wills and estate documents, naturalization papers, and some vital records, take the time to try to obtain copies of the actual records by contacting the repository in writing.

Organize Everything Sequentially

Collate the evidence copies for the individual into chronological sequence. Arrange materials in order based on the event or action that each is documenting. For example, start with the census for the parents of the individual before that person was born. Follow that with a birth certificate, a christening record, school registration or attendance records, marriage license and certificate (or copy recorded in a county marriage book), military service records, employment information, a Social Security application (SS-5), real estate and tax records, and so on. Include each census throughout the person's life or alternate records, such as city directories and voter registration records, to establish location at every point in time. Don't stop with a death certificate or similar document. A death announcement, obituary, and/or funeral notice is filled with details. Be sure to include undertaker details and burial information. Continue to the will and probate records, including probate court minutes, and everything included in the estate papers until the estate is settled and distribution is made to heirs. If you are missing any of documents, and others you may think were produced during the person's lifetime, make the effort to locate and obtain exact copies of them.

Reread Everything

Because evidence comes to you in different forms and at different times, it is essential to reread everything—in chronological sequence—as if you have never seen any of the evidence before. Your knowledge of record types and research has grown over time and, when you reread the materials this time, the content details that meant little or nothing before may suddenly take on a new significance. It will not be unusual to find yourself flipping back and forth through the evidence in front of you because some small detail piques your interest to help fill in a longstanding gap. Newly discovered clues can lead you to new source materials.

Compile a Timeline

Your next step is to create an ancestor timeline. Use a word processor or spreadsheet program to produce a template with columns for:

- **Date**   Indicate year or year/month/day.
- **Description and source citation**   You will type a textual description of the information or event for each piece of evidence, along with a source citation describing where the information originated and where you obtained it. If you have multiple pieces of evidence for the

same fact, include each one and its source citation. You want to compare each piece of evidence to determine what it tells you *and* how strong the source is. If two sources present conflicting information, you will want to address the discrepancy.

After creating the chronological timeline for the person, proofread it for errors. Then read it as the biographical outline it is. You will then want to add more information to this person's profile timeline.

■ **Information about other family members**   You will want to add entries about other people who may have influenced your ancestor and their life events. The deaths of parents can be life-changing events. The births, marriages, and deaths of siblings and children are important. Details about migrations and other personal events will add important context to your ancestor's story.

■ **Historical and social events**   You should also study local, county, state, country, and world history to identify events that may have influenced your ancestor and his or her family. That will include historical events in which your ancestor may have participated, in all areas of the world in which they lived, or which affected their lives. Military conflicts that affected Americans have included the American Revolution, the War of 1812, the Indian Wars, the U.S. Civil War, the Spanish American War, World War I, World War II, the Korean War, the Vietnam War, and others. Economic depressions, such as the one in the 1930s; epidemics, such as the 1918 influenza pandemic; famines, such those in Ireland in 1740–1741 and the 1840s; natural disasters, such as earthquakes, floods, tornadoes, and hurricanes; emigration/immigration surges; and other events are very important influences. Don't overlook changes in governments and changes in political boundaries over time, as these cause significant cultural changes.

The following is an abbreviated example of an ancestor profile for George's great-grandmother, Caroline Alice Whitefield. This illustrates how such a document can be created.

Caroline Alice WHITEFIELD/WHITFIELD
(23 August 1853 – 26 June 1917)

YEAR	EVENT
1850	Parents, William Whitfield [sic Whitefield] and Sophia [nee Sophia D. Briggs] resided in Person County, North Carolina, in the 1850 U.S. federal census.
	Sources: ■ Year: *1850*; Census Place: *Person, North Carolina*; Roll: *M432_640*; Page: *418A*; Image: *251*. ■ Ancestry.com. *1850 United States Federal Census* [database online]. Provo, Utah, USA: Ancestry.com Operations, Inc., 2009. Images reproduced by FamilySearch.
1853	Born 23 August 1853 in Bushy Fork Township, Person County, North Carolina.
	Sources: ■ Caswell County Death Certificate # 321. "North Carolina, Deaths, 1906-1930," index and images, *FamilySearch*(https://familysearch.org/pal:/MM9.1.1/F-N4W: accessed 29 March 2013), Caroline Alice Carter, 26 June 1917. ■ Entry in Bible belonging to Laura Augusta "Minnie" Wilson Morgan Bible. In possession of George G. Morgan, [street address, city, state, and ZIP code] as of 29 March 2013. ■ Tombstone. Findagrave.com, Cooper Cemetery, Ridgeville, Caswell County, North Carolina. Memorial #27301763.
1857	Father, William A. Whitefield, died on 18 September 1857 in Roxboro, Person County, North Carolina.
	Sources: ■ North Carolina Estate Files, 1663–1979, Person County, W, Whitfield, William (1858)—41 images. "North Carolina, Estate Files, 1663–1979," index and images, FamilySearch.org (https://familysearch.org/pal:/MM9.1.1/KDGN-BN8: accessed 29 March 2013), William Whitfield, 1858. ■ Findagrave.com, Memorial #38348337. Gravestone shows birth and death dates.
1857	Thomas H. Briggs was appointed guardian of Frances Whitefield, Preston Whitefield, Malcolm Whitefield, and Caroline A. Whitefield on 22 December 1857.
	Source: ■ North Carolina Estate Files, 1663–1979, Person County, W, Whitfield, William (1858–1861)—image 40. "North Carolina, Estate Files, 1663–1979," index and images, *FamilySearch* (https://familysearch.org/pal:/MM9.1.1/KDGN-BN8: accessed 29 March 2013), William Whitfield, 1858.
1859	Mother, Sophia D. [Briggs] Whitefield, died on 29 April 1859 in Roxboro, Person County, North Carolina.
	Source: ■ North Carolina Estate Files, 1663–1979, Person County, W, Whitfield, Sophia (1858–1861)—8 images. "North Carolina, Estate Files, 1663–1979," index and images, *FamilySearch* (https://familysearch.org/pal:/MM9.1.1/KDGN-BN4: accessed 29 March 2013), Sophia Whitfield, no date.

YEAR	EVENT
1860	1860 U.S. federal census—Caroline A. Whitefield is found in home of Adolphus Villines and wife Emily in Person County, North Carolina. (At the time of this writing, Caroline's surname is misindexed by Ancestry.com as Aschelefed.)

Source:
- Ancestry.com. *1860 United States Federal Census* [database online]. Provo, Utah, USA: Ancestry.com Operations, Inc., 2009. Images reproduced by FamilySearch.

YEAR	EVENT
1860	1860 U.S. federal census—slave schedules—Frances Whitefield and Caroline A. Whitefield are found to own slaves. There is a notation on the schedule that "Dolphin Villines Guardian for" Frances Whitefield and Caroline Whitefield.

Sources:
- Ancestry.com. *1860 U.S. Federal Census—Slave Schedules* [database online]. Provo, Utah, USA: Ancestry.com Operations Inc, 2010.
- Original data: United States of America, Bureau of the Census. *Eighth Census of the United States, 1860*. Washington, D.C.: National Archives and Records Administration, 1860. M653, 1,438 rolls.

YEAR	EVENT
1861	Support payment made from estate of Sophia Whitefield to D. D. Villines for support of Frances Whitefield and Caroline Alice Whitefield.

Source:
- North Carolina Estate Files, 1663–1979, Person County, W, Whitfield, Sophia (1858–1861)—8 images. "North Carolina, Estate Files, 1663–1979," index and images, *FamilySearch* (https://familysearch.org/pal:/MM9.1.1/KDGN-BN4: accessed 29 March 2013), Sophia Whitfield, no date.

YEAR	EVENT
1870	1870 U.S. federal census—Caroline Whitefield is found in Bushy Fork Township, Person County, North Carolina in the home of Dolphin D. Villines and his wife Emily, and Emily Villines (age 80).

Sources:
- Ancestry.com. *1870 United States Federal Census* [database online]. Provo, Utah, USA: Ancestry.com Operations, Inc., 2009. Images reproduced by FamilySearch.
- 1870 U.S. census, population schedules. NARA microfilm publication M593, 1,761 rolls. Washington, D.C.: National Archives and Records Administration, no date.

YEAR	EVENT
1871	Marriage to Rainey Baines Morgan on 19 November 1871 in Caswell County, North Carolina.

Source:
- Caswell County Marriage Book H, Caswell County Courthouse, 144 Court Square, Yanceyville, North Carolina.

YEAR	EVENT
1879	Samuel Goodloe Morgan was born on 6 April 1879 in Caswell County, North Carolina.

Sources:
- 1900 U.S. federal census, Hightowers Township, Caswell County, North Carolina. Ancestry.com. *1900 United States Federal Census* [database online]. Provo, Utah, USA: Ancestry.com Operations Inc, 2004.
- Original data: United States of America, Bureau of the Census. *Twelfth Census of the United States, 1900*. Washington, D.C.: National Archives and Records Administration, 1900. T623, 1854 rolls.
- Tombstone. Findagrave.com, Woodland Cemetery, Madison, Rockingham County, North Carolina. Memorial #26916367.
- Entry in Bible belonging to Laura Augusta "Minnie" Wilson Morgan Bible. In possession of [add residential address here] as of 29 March 2013.

YEAR	EVENT
1880	1880 U.S. federal census, Hightowers, Caswell County, North Carolina. R. B. Morgan, C. A. Morgan, and S. G. Morgan are living in the home of G. W. Morgan and his wife, M. L. Morgan.
	Sources: ■ Ancestry.com and The Church of Jesus Christ of Latter-day Saints. *1880 United States Federal Census* [database online]. Provo, Utah, USA: Ancestry.com Operations Inc, 2010. 1880 U.S. Census Index provided by The Church of Jesus Christ of Latter-day Saints © Copyright 1999, Intellectual Reserve, Inc. All rights reserved. All use is subject to the limited use license and other terms and conditions applicable to this site. ■ Original data: Tenth Census of the United States, 1880. (NARA microfilm publication T9, 1,454 rolls). Records of the Bureau of the Census, Record Group 29. National Archives, Washington, D.C.
1881	William Rainey Morgan was born on 26 June 1881 in Caswell County, North Carolina.
	Sources: ■ 1900 U.S. federal census, Hightowers Township, Caswell County, North Carolina. Ancestry.com. *1900 United States Federal Census* [database online]. Provo, Utah, USA: Ancestry.com Operations Inc, 2004. ■ Tombstone. Findagrave.com, Cooper Cemetery, Ridgeville, Caswell County, North Carolina. Memorial #53570431.
1883	There was a purchase by Rainey Baines Morgan and wife, Caroline A. Morgan, from Goodlow Warren Morgan of a tract of land of approximately 271.5 acres. Purchase price was $4900. The transaction was dated 16 May 1883. Recorded in the Caswell County, North Carolina, Deed Book RR, page 161. Husband's and wife's signatures can be seen on the original copy in the possession of George G. Morgan.
1883	John Allen Morgan was born on 5 November 1883 in Caswell County, North Carolina.
	Sources: 1900 U.S. federal census, Hightowers Township, Caswell County, North Carolina. Ancestry.com. *1900 United States Federal Census* [database online]. Provo, Utah, USA: Ancestry.com Operations Inc, 2004. Tombstone. Findagrave.com, Cooper Cemetery, Ridgeville, Caswell County, North Carolina. Memorial #92078648.
1891	Husband, Rainey Baines Morgan, died on 13 September 1891 of infection.
	Sources: ■ Entry in Bible belonging to Samuel Goodloe Morgan Bible. In possession of George G. Morgan, [enter residential address] as of 29 March 2013. ■ Tombstone. Findagrave.com, Cooper Cemetery, Ridgeville, Caswell County, North Carolina. Memorial #52883752.
1893	On 8 April 1893, Caroline A. Morgan filed a Petition for Dower in Caswell County, North Carolina, against "Samuel G. Morgan. Wm. R. Morgan, John A. Morgan, in fact under twenty one years of age," and G. W. Morgan because her husband, Rainey B. Morgan, had died intestate. This is recorded in Book B of Orders and Decrees, pages 363 and 364. (This was part of her dower petition documentation.)

YEAR	EVENT
1893	Married Thomas Jehu Carter on 19 November 1893 in Caswell County, North Carolina.

Source:
- "North Carolina, Marriages, 1759–1979," index, *FamilySearch* (https://familysearch.org/pal:/MM9.1.1/F8DL-SGL: accessed 29 March 2013), Thomas J. Carter and Caroline Morgan, 19 November 1893.

1902	Samuel Goodloe Morgan married Laura Augusta "Minnie" Wilson Murphy [a widow] on 24 December 1902 at Lemley, Mecklenburg County, North Carolina.

Sources:
- "North Carolina, Marriages, 1759–1979," index, *FamilySearch* (https://familysearch.org/pal:/MM9.1.1/F8WD-HJS: accessed 29 March 2013), S. G. Morgan and Mrs. Minnie Murphy, 24 December 1902.
- Entry in Bible belonging to Laura Augusta "Minnie" Wilson Morgan Bible. In possession of George G. Morgan, [enter residential address] as of 29 March 2013.
  - Children:
    - Mary Allen Morgan (14 June 1909–19 February 1969)
    - Samuel Thomas Morgan (18 December 1909–2 May 1980)

1903	William Rainey Morgan married Lessie Thaxton on 4 November 1903 at Hightowers, Caswell County, North Carolina.

Source:
- "North Carolina, Marriages, 1759-1979," index, *FamilySearch* (https://familysearch.org/pal:/MM9.1.1/F8FS-PLX: accessed 29 March 2013), W. R. Morgan and Lessie Thaxton, 4 November 1903.
  - Children:
    - Henry Carter Morgan (10 April 1905–15 January 1907)
    - William Rainey Morgan, Jr. (11 June 1906–24 August 1988)
    - Irene Kate Morgan (4 October 1909–2 April 1950)
    - Mae Alice Morgan (1 May 1914–15 October 1987)
    - Henry Speck Morgan (12 October 1917–16 September 2008)
    - Margaret Caroline Morgan (23 April 1923–3 April 2012)

1910	John Allen Morgan married Flora May Wrenn on 27 December 1910 in Siler City, Chatham County, North Carolina.

Source:
- "North Carolina, Marriages, 1759–1979," index, *FamilySearch* (https://familysearch.org/pal:/MM9.1.1/F8XD-GGT: accessed 29 March 2013), John A. Morgan and Flora May Wrenn, 27 December 1910.
  - Children:
    - Alice May Morgan (7 April 1914 – 15 April 1914)
    - John Wrenn Morgan (6 July 1916 – 9 March 1979)

YEAR	EVENT
1917	Died 26 June 1917 at Prospect Hill, Caswell County, North Carolina, of liver cancer. Age 63 years, 10 months, 3 days.
	Sources: ■ Caswell County Death Certificate # 321. "North Carolina, Deaths, 1906–1930," index and images, *FamilySearch* (https://familysearch.org/pal:/MM9.1.1/F3CM-N4W: accessed 29 March 2013), Caroline Alice Carter, 26 June 1917. ■ Entry in Bible belonging to Laura Augusta "Minnie" Wilson Morgan Bible. In possession of George G. Morgan, [enter residential address] as of 29 March 2013. ■ Entry in Bible belonging to Samuel Goodloe Morgan Bible. In possession of George G. Morgan, [enter residential address] as of 29 March 2013. ■ Tombstone. Findagrave.com, Cooper Cemetery, Ridgeville, Caswell County, North Carolina. Memorial #27301763.
1917	Buried in Cooper Cemetery at Ridgeville, Caswell County, North Carolina, after 26 June 1917.
	Sources: ■ Tombstone. Findagrave.com, Cooper Cemetery, Ridgeville, Caswell County, North Carolina. Memorial #27301763. ■ Personal visit and photographs.

Incorporate Historical Newspaper Research

Supplement your knowledge of historical events *and* about your specific ancestor by researching historical newspapers. Massive collections of digitized and indexed newspapers are available through public and academic libraries' and archives' institutional subscriptions to such resources as NewsBank, inc.'s America's GenealogyBank and America's Obituaries & Death Notices databases, the ProQuest Historical Newspaper databases, and others. You may also personally subscribe to the British Newspaper Archive (http://www.britishnewspaperarchive .co.uk), GenealogyBank (http://www.genealogybank.com), NewspaperArchive.com (http://www.newspaperarchive.com), and Newspapers.com (http://www.newspapers.com), and you can access newspapers as part of paid subscriptions to Ancestry .com (http://www.ancestry.com), findmypast.com (http:// www.findmypast.com), World Vital Records (http://www .worldvitalrecords.com), and others.

Let's look at some examples of the concepts we've discussed in this chapter.

Example 1

You can learn a great deal about individuals, family groups, and other individuals sharing the same residence by using U.S. federal census population schedules. The census is certainly the most used document by genealogists, who use these materials to place people into a specific geographical area and gather other important personal information. It is a common mistake, however, to use only one year's census document in researching an individual. Different censuses asked different questions, and the responses to those can expand your knowledge about individuals. You may also find discrepancies in the responses to the same question asked on multiple censuses. Census records can be problematic for the following reasons:

- The enumerator may not have asked the questions in a way that the respondent understood. The respondent may not have spoken English well or at all, and may have provided incorrect information.

- The enumerator may have asked questions of a neighbor or someone who was not a member of the family.

- The respondent may have remembered details of some events and forgotten or misremembered others. Dates, ages, and locations may have become muddled with the passage of time.

- The respondent may not have known the answers to a question, or may have intentionally lied.

As a result, census records should always be considered as secondary sources of information, except for the fact of residence itself. They provide clues to be followed but need to be verified using other resources, preferably original primary source documentation. Census records should also be studied as a group. For example, locate every census record for an individual or family and chart each person over an entire lifetime if possible.

Our first brick wall example involves the family of Louis and Sarah Weinglass. We want to examine the family in the U.S. federal census population schedules of 1900 through 1930 to see what we can learn that might point us elsewhere.

The 1900 U.S. federal census, details from which are shown in Figures 1-4a and 1-4b, shows us that Louis Weinglass was born in February 1864 in Russia of Russian parents. He is now 36 years old. He states that he arrived in the United States in 1876 and has been here 24 years, and that he is a naturalized citizen. His wife, Sarah, is shown as having been born in March 1871 in Russia, also of Russian parents. She is 29 years old. She arrived in 1884, 16 years ago, and is not naturalized. The couple has been married for 13 years, implying a marriage in 1887, and they have had six children, all of whom were born in New Jersey and are still living. Louis is employed as an agent of a sewing machine company. Both Louis and Sarah can read, write, and speak English.

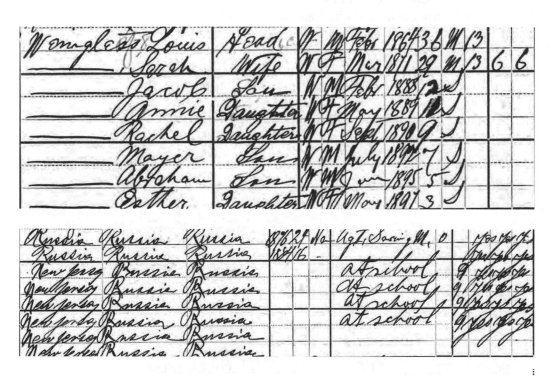

Figure 1-4 a and 4b 1900 U.S. federal census—Newark City, Essex County, New Jersey (by permission of Ancestry.com)

A search for naturalization records for Louis at Ancestry.com yields an index card for his naturalization on 14 October 1890. (See Figure 1-5.) Further research for his naturalization documents would probably yield his petition for naturalization, including his date and port of arrival, the name of the ship on which he traveled, and his renunciation of the country of his previous citizenship.

We performed a search for marriage records for all Weinglass groom records at the Stephen P. Morse New York City Groom Index in One Step at http://stevemorse.org/vital/nymarriages.html?index=groom. The search results yielded ten matches. Two of these were for Lewis Weinglass and Louis Weinglass with the same marriage certificate number 70185 in Manhattan dated 24 May 1887. Clicking on the bride link showed her name as Sara Levy.

The 1910 census, details of which are shown in Figures 1-6a and 1-6b, finds Sarah renting a home at another address in the same area of Newark. She is now widowed, the mother of eight children, all of whom are still living. Seven of those children live with her. The oldest son, Jacob, is no longer at home. Notice several differences in this census. Sarah and her parents are listed as Russian Yiddish. There are variations in the children's names: Annie is now called Anna, Rachel

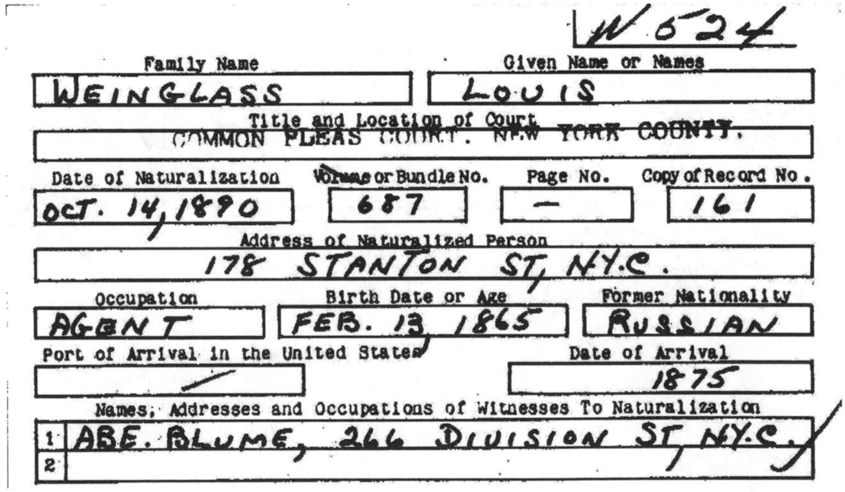

W 524

Family Name: WEINGLASS
Given Name or Names: LOUIS
Title and Location of Court: COMMON PLEAS COURT. NEW YORK COUNTY.
Date of Naturalization: OCT. 14, 1890
Volume or Bundle No.: 687
Page No.: —
Copy of Record No.: 161
Address of Naturalized Person: 178 STANTON ST, N.Y.C.
Occupation: AGENT
Birth Date or Age: FEB. 13, 1865
Former Nationality: RUSSIAN
Port of Arrival in the United States: —
Date of Arrival: 1875
Names, Addresses and Occupations of Witnesses To Naturalization
1 ABE. BLUME, 266 DIVISION ST, N.Y.C.
2

FIGURE 1-5 Index card for the naturalization documents for Louis Weinglass (by permission of Ancestry.com)

Weinglass	Sarah	Head—OT	F	W	41	Wd		8	8
	Anna	Daughter	F	W	20	S			
	Ray	Daughter	F	W	19	S			
	Esther	Daughter	F	W	12	S			
	Delia	Daughter	F	W	7	S			
	Meyer	Son	M	W	17	S			
	Abraham	Son	M	W	15	S			
	Saul	Son	M	W	9	S			

Russ. Yiddish	Russ. Yiddish	Russ. Yiddish	1881	Na	English	None		
New York	Russ. Yiddish	Russ. Yiddish			English	Keeper	Stationary store
New York	Russ. Yiddish	Russ. Yiddish			English	Operator	Underground
Tennessee	Russ. Yiddish	Russ. Yiddish			English	Renovation	Automobile Factory
New York	Russ. Yiddish	Russ. Yiddish			English	None	
New York	Russ. Yiddish	Russ. Yiddish			English	None	
New York	Russ. Yiddish	Russ. Yiddish			English	Apprentice	Painter shop
Tennessee	Russ. Yiddish	Russ. Yiddish			English	None	

FIGURE 1-6 A AND 6B 1910 U.S. federal census—Newark City (part of), Essex County, New Jersey (by permission of Ancestry.com)

is now called Ray, and Mayer is now spelled Meyer. Two children, Saul and Delia, were born after the 1900 census. You will also note that the place of birth of some children has changed. Four of the five remaining children who were in the household in 1910 are listed as born in New York, and not in New Jersey. Esther is now listed as born in Tennessee, rather than New Jersey. Saul, age 9, is shown as born in Tennessee and Delia, age 7, was born in New York.

This information now points to birth records for the children in New York, rather than New Jersey, and to two births in Tennessee. Louis was an agent for a sewing machine company. It is possible that Sarah and perhaps the whole family lived in Tennessee at some time. Statewide legislation requiring registration of births, marriages, and deaths was not passed until 1914, but delayed birth certificates and other substitute documents may establish Esther's and Saul's births in Tennessee.

Sarah states in 1910 that she arrived in the United States in 1881 and that she now is naturalized. (See details in Figure 1-7.) She is the keeper of a stationery store. This should prompt a search in New York or New Jersey for her naturalization papers.

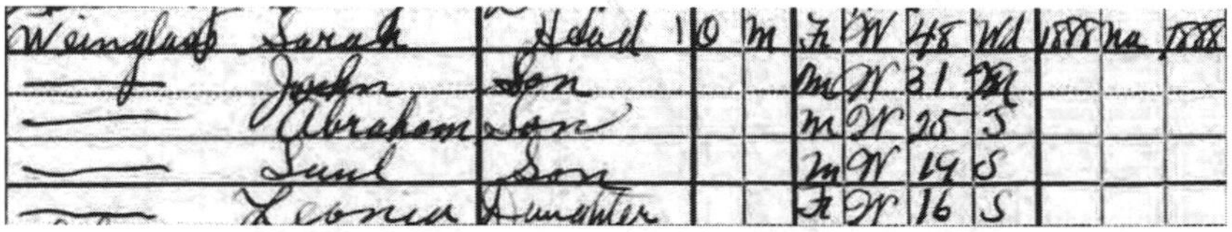

Weinglast	Sarah	Head	1	O	M	F	W	48	Wd	1888	Na	1888
—	John	Son				M	W	31	M			
—	Abraham	Son				M	W	25	S			
—	Saul	Son				M	W	19	S			
—	Leonia	Daughter				F	W	16	S			

Figure 1-7 1920 U.S. federal census—Newark City, Essex County, New Jersey (by permission of Ancestry.com)

Note We must be certain to check her husband's naturalization papers to verify whether or not she received derivative naturalization through his naturalization process.

Sarah appears in the 1920 census at 55 Fleming Avenue in a home that she owns on a mortgage. She is the storekeeper of a hardware store. Three children live with her. John, age 31, is home and listed as married. (It appears that the enumerator originally wrote "Jack" and then wrote "John" on top of it. He is the oldest son, previously known as Jacob.) Sons Abraham (25) and Saul (19) are also present, as is a daughter, Leonia (16) who is likely the daughter named Delia in the 1920 census.

Sarah's year of arrival in the United States is listed as 1888, and she is listed as naturalized in the same year. The year of arrival is improbable as she and Louis state in 1900 that they have been married for 13 years, and Jacob is listed as having been born in February 1888. Since she is listed as naturalized, it would be wise to search for her in New Jersey and New York naturalization indexes.

The 1930 census, detail of which is shown in Figures 1-8a and 1-8b, shows Sarah in a home she owns with a mortgage in Kearny, New Jersey. The home is a duplex valued at $8,000, and she rents part to Robert Watters and his family for $45 per month.

Four other people live with Sarah in the 1930 census. Anna is 37 years old and listed as divorced, and having been married at age 20. She is using her maiden name. Dora, age 32 and single, is likely Esther. Sadie, age 25 and single, may be Delia/Leonia. Irvin is listed as 17, and he cannot be one of Sarah's children. He may be Anna's son or he may be a nephew. Additional research would be required into other family groups.

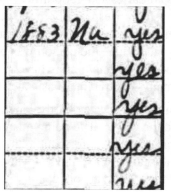

FIGURE 1-8 A AND 8B 1930 U.S. federal census—Kearny Town, Hudson County, New Jersey (by permission of Ancestry.com)

Sarah's year of arrival is listed this time as 1883, and she indicates that she is naturalized. The conflicting years of arrival in the various censuses should be further researched.

The review of Sarah and her family in four census population schedules revealed a number of discrepancies. These variants need to be carefully examined, and they may yield other details to help demolish a brick wall.

- Name variations can help refocus research on alternate spellings and name changes (legal or casual) that can generate brick walls.

- Birth dates and ages shown on census records are often different than reality. Some people may not know their date and year of birth or they misremember them. Others may lie about their ages. Remember, too, that census day varied from decade to decade. Ages shown on census records should reflect the age at the last birthday, and a 9-year or 11-year difference is not uncommon when taking the official census date into consideration.

- Place of birth may become confused, especially among families who moved often. The proximity of a residence to a state line, in this case the proximity of northern New Jersey to the New York City metropolitan area, may have been confusing to some people, causing them to misremember exactly where they were when. Changes in boundaries and geopolitical jurisdictions need to be considered, especially in the country of birth. Enumerators may have asked for the current name of the place where the person was born. Someone born in Poland, for example, may have responded with Poland, Germany, Austria, or Russia at different times.

- Differences in the stated date of arrival in the United States may be due to the correct date being misremembered. It is also possible that the informant to the census taker may have confused the year of arrival with a year that the family took a trip back to the old country.

You can see that relying on only one census can result in erroneous information that leads you down the wrong research path.

Example 2

A death notice, obituary, or funeral notice is a small biographical sketch about the life of someone who has died, and genealogists use obituaries as clues to additional evidence. Many researchers, after referring to an obituary the first time, file a copy and don't revisit the content.

As you continue your research over time, you gather new evidence and gain more insight into an individual's life and/or those of other family members. You may continue the quest until you reach a brick wall. It then becomes imperative that you reread every piece of evidence that you have acquired over time and place every event into geographical and historical context.

It is useful to create an ancestor profile or timeline for in-depth review. You can begin by arranging all of the evidential sources you have into chronological order. Create a document for an individual's facts that includes columns for a date, location, a description of the evidence, and a source citation.

Create an entry for every piece of information gleaned from the each source. You may have multiple entries from the same piece of evidence, even if some of the data is less reliable, secondary information. For example, a death certificate may provide information about an individual's name, date of birth, parents' names, spouse's name, date of death, name of funeral home or mortuary, date of burial, and interment location. Some of these items may be incorrect if the informant wasn't knowledgeable or if the passage of time had blurred the accuracy of names, dates, and locations. The entries should be associated with a date and entered in chronological sequence.

Remember that an obituary is an important piece of documentation, even if the data may be less than 100 percent accurate. It is essential that the obituary be used as a source *after* you have created entries for all other source evidence. An obituary can be dissected to identify each potential fact and help identify where and how to acquire more information. Figure 1-9 shows a dissection of an obituary and the potential

FIGURE 1-9 Obituary for Mr. Francis M. Stocks of Atlanta, Georgia (by permission of ProQuest)

Obituary 3 -- No Title
The Atlanta Constitution (1881-1945); Jun 27, 1918;
ProQuest Historical Newspapers: The Atlanta Constitution (1868-1945)
pg. 10

F. M. Stocks, Pioneer
Resident of Atlanta,
Dies at Residence

Francis M. Stocks, a pioneer resident of Atlanta and one of the city's most prominent men, died at 4 o'clock Wednesday afternoon at his home on Piedmont road at the age of 68 years.

Mr. Stocks came to Atlanta in 1880, was founder and proprietor of the Stocks Coal company, and conducted a prosperous business for 38 years. He was a Christian gentleman and a member of the Walker Street M. E. church since he first came to Atlanta. He was always ready to give to charitable work and to help those in need.

Mr. Stocks had a slight stroke of paralysis seven years ago, when his wife died, and has never been himself since. In April he had his second stroke, and he had been very low until his death Wednesday.

He is survived by five children, Thomas F. Stocks, Miss Nellie Stocks, Mrs. Gerald G. Hannah, Mrs. Alvis M. Weatherly of Birmingham, and Mrs. W. Watts Morgan, and two brothers, James D. Stocks and William H. Stocks.

Funeral arrangements will be announced later.

clues that can point to new evidence. This new evidence may then fill in blanks in the person's life and can potentially open still other research avenues.

The obituary for Mr. Francis M. Stocks of Atlanta, Georgia, shown in Table 1-1, can be dissected to identify the following information. The first piece of information to be gleaned is the publication, *The Atlanta Constitution*, and date of publication, June 27, 1918.

Text	Information	Inferred Clue	New Data Location
HEADLINE: F M. Stocks	Name.	One method of address.	Use for alternate searches of other records.
HEADLINE: Pioneer Resident of Atlanta	Long residence in Atlanta.	Other older records may exist.	State and local histories; city directories.
HEADLINE: Dies at Residence	Died at home.	Probably died in Atlanta.	City directories for 1917 and 1918; property records for the residence.
Francis M. Stocks	Full spelling of forename.	Another method of address.	Use for alternate searches of other records.
a pioneer resident of Atlanta	Same as headline.	Same as headline.	Same as headline.
and one of the city's most prominent men	Indicates that he was well-known and respected.	Potentially involved in many civic affairs.	Search historic newspapers for other stories.
died at 4 o'clock Wednesday afternoon	Date of death.	Using publication date, this determines the date of death to have been Wednesday, 26 June 1918.	Search *The Historic Atlanta Constitution* newspaper database for more information on later dates. Use perpetual calendar to determine day of the week for this newspaper item, and calculate date on Wednesday. Search for death certificate and related records.
at his home on Piedmont road	Location of the individual's home.	More precisely identify residence address.	City directories for 1917 and 1918; property records for the residence (grantee and grantor indexes and deeds).

TABLE 1-1   Dissection of the obituary of Francis M. Stocks (*continued*)

Text	Information	Inferred Clue	New Data Location
at the age of 68 years	Individual's age.	Individual was born circa 1850.	Search 1900 census and determine date of birth was 1850 in Georgia (and other family members' information).
Mr. Stocks came to Atlanta in 1880,	Year of arrival in the community.	Was elsewhere prior to arrival in Atlanta.	Search other censuses for Georgia and surrounding states for prior location(s) and occupation(s).
was founder of the Stocks Coal company, and conducted a prosperous business for 38 years.	Occupation and duration of his involvement.	Determine location and scope of the business.	Search historical newspapers, city directories, business directories, and other materials related this individual and to the coal industry.
He was a Christian gentleman and a member of the Walker Street M. E. church since he first came to Atlanta.	Identity of his church and its location.	Use church membership records to determine the church and location from which he may have transferred membership. Identify church where he was married.	Contact church for copies of membership records and other documents.
He was always ready to give to charitable work and to help those in need.	Describes something of his nature.	Charitable donations, both personal and business, may be documented.	Search historical newspapers for stories. Ask church about charitable support.
Mr. Stocks had a slight stroke seven years ago, when his wife died, and has never been the same since.	Describes a physical health problem. Refers to his wife's death seven years ago.	Infers a possible date for his withdrawal from his coal business. Points to information about his wife's death circa 1911.	Search historical newspapers for an obituary for Mrs. Stocks.
In April he had his second stroke, and he had been very low until his death on Wednesday.	Describes a second stroke and the time period. States the day of the week of his death.	Verifies the day of the week of his death.	Use perpetual calendar to determine day of the week for this newspaper item, and calculate date on Wednesday.

TABLE 1-1   Dissection of the obituary of Francis M. Stocks (*continued*)

Text	Information	Inferred Clue	New Data Location
He is survived by five children, Thomas F. Stocks, Miss Nellie Stocks, Mrs. Gerald G. Hannah, Mrs. Alvis M. Weatherly of Birmingham [Alabama], and Mrs. W. Watts Morgan,	Defines the names of his five surviving children.	Names of sons and daughters without a specified location imply that they are local. Mrs. Weatherly is the only surviving child from outside the vicinity.	Search censuses for all children's names. Search for marriage records/licenses in Atlanta, Fulton County, Georgia, area, and in the Birmingham area as these may provide the links between husbands and daughters.
two brothers, James D. Stocks and William H. Stocks	Defines names of surviving siblings.	Can help locate the parents of Francis and his two brothers.	Search census records for the brothers going back in time until parents may be located and identified. Search records of brothers to help identify parents and other members of the Stocks family.
Funeral arrangements will be announced later.	This is the death notice for Francis M. Stocks.	Other newspaper notices, such as a more detailed obituary and a funeral notice, may be available.	Search historical newspapers for additional death-related notices. Search later newspapers for notices published by the executor/administrator of his estate. Search for probate court records, including probate packet contents and probate court minutes. Search grantee indexes in Fulton County to determine transfer of real property to heirs.

TABLE 1-1   Dissection of the obituary of Francis M. Stocks

Dissecting the published death notice, obituary, or funeral notice, as shown in Table 1-1, can provide invaluable clues to information you may not have thought to search for before. Be certain to look for multiple notices in several days' newspapers and in other newspapers elsewhere. The details published in each notice may be slightly more concise or different. Remember that the later the notice, the better the chance that earlier incorrect data may have been corrected.

After reviewing and dissecting the obituary publications, follow through on the new details they provide or imply. You can add entries to your biographical profile or timeline for each new event you find. In addition, you can add entries for other related family members' events and for historical events that may have influenced the individual's life. All of this information will construct the geographical, historical, and personal context to expand your knowledge. You can see why reexamining obituaries can be extremely helpful in gathering new information that can restart research stalled by a brick wall.

Example 3

Goal   Locate Caroline A. Whitefield, born 23 August 1853, in the 1860 U.S. federal census. Identify the maiden name of the wife of William Whitefield and Caroline's mother.

What Has Already Been Researched?

- ■ The vital dates of Caroline Alice Whitefield (23 August 1853 to 26 June 1917) are shown on her tombstone (see Figure 1-10). She has been identified as the daughter of William and Sophia Whitefield (sometimes spelled Whitfield).

FIGURE 1-10 Tombstone of Caroline Alice Whitefield Morgan Carter

- The 1850 U.S. federal census shows William Whitfield, aged 51, and Sophia, aged 38, living with eight children, ages 23 years to 11 months. Caroline had not yet been born.

- William Whitefield died on 18 September 1857 in Roxboro, Caswell County, North Carolina. His will, dated 8 November 1856, is included in Caswell County Will Book R, and references his wife as "Sophia Whitefield."

- Unable to locate Caroline Whitefield (white female) in the 1860 U.S. federal census population schedules.

- Located Caroline Whitefield (aged 18) in the 1870 U.S. federal census (Ancestry.com) in Bushy Fork Township, Person County, North Carolina, the home of Dolphin D. Villines (aged 52), Emily (aged 49), and Sallie (aged 80).

- She was the wife of Rainey Baines Morgan (27 November 1851 to 13 September 1891). The couple married on 19 November 1871 as evidenced in Caswell County, North Carolina, marriage records. They had three sons: Samuel Goodloe Morgan, William Rainey Morgan, and John Allen Morgan.

- After Morgan's death, Caroline remarried. She wed Thomas J. Carter on 19 November 1893 in Caswell County, North Carolina.

How We Solved the Brick Wall

- Reexamined the 1870 U.S. federal census at Ancestry. com for Bushy Fork Township, Person County, North Carolina, and located the home of Dolphin D. Villines. He was 52 years old. Living with him were Emily (aged 49), Sallie (aged 80), and Caroline Whitefield (18).

- Reexamined the 1860 U.S. federal census population schedules at Ancestry.com and searched for Dolphin Villines without success. Searched for Emily and Sally without success. Searched using the exact, Soundex, phonetic, and similar sounds or spellings without success. Searched for Caroline Whitefield or Whitfield without success.

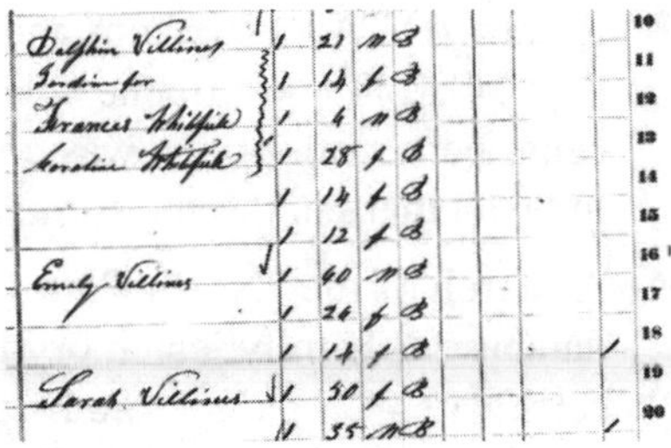

FIGURE 1-11 1860 U.S. federal census slave schedule showing Caroline Whitefield (Ancestry.com image)

■ Searched the 1860 U.S. federal census slave schedules at Ancestry.com and located Dolphin Villines in Person County, North Carolina, and a notation that he is guardian for Frances Whitefield and Caroline Whitefield. (See Figure 1-11.) Emily Villines and Sally Villines are also listed.

■ Checked the census index at findmypast.com and, using additional searches with spelling variations, located Adolphus Vellins (aged 44) and Emily Vellins (42). Frances Whitfield (16) and Caroline A. Whitefed (7) (indexed based on poor handwriting) are indexed and shown, along with Frances Briggs (age 81), Sarah Vellins (74), Emily H. Vellins (15), and Judah Bush (40), Lewis Bush (12), Haywood Bush (12), and Nelson Bush (2). Frances Briggs and Sarah Vellins are likely the parents, respectively, of Emily and Adolphus, respectively. (See Figure 1-12.)

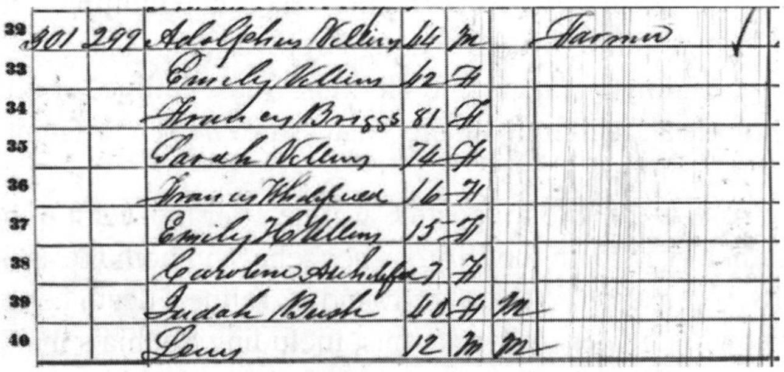

FIGURE 1-12 1860 U.S. federal census population schedule for the Adolphus Vellins household showing Caroline's entry (by permission of findmypast.com)

- Returned to Ancestry.com and located the census record there. Caroline's surname was poorly written by the census enumerator and was consequently incorrectly indexed there under the surname of Aschelefed.

- A search of the "North Carolina, Deaths, 1906–1930" database at FamilySearch.org located Caroline's death certificate. Her parents are listed as William Whitefield and Sophia Briggs, both of Person County, North Carolina. Caroline's place of birth is listed as Bushy Fork in Person County, North Carolina, and the informant is S. G. Morgan, her eldest son by her first marriage.

- A marriage bond signed by William Whitefield and Dolphin Villines on 30 July 1842 in Person County, shown in Figure 1-13, states that William Whitefield is applying for an application to marry Sophia D. Briggs. It is indexed in the FamilySearch.org database, "North Carolina Marriages 1759–1979." A copy of the image was obtained from Family History Library microfilm 6330326. A search of this same database for Dolphin Villines shows another marriage bond entry for him and Emily L. Briggs on the same date, suggesting that there may have been a double marriage.

FIGURE 1-13 Marriage bond between William Whitefield and Dolphin Villines (by permission of FamilySearch.org)

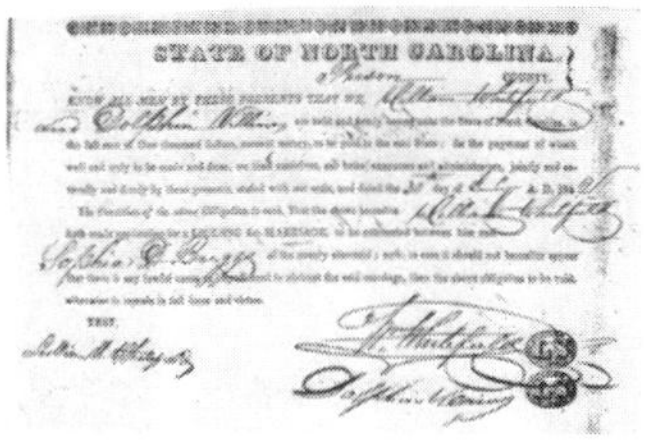

What Broke the Brick Wall

Census indexing is notoriously difficult because the enumerators misspelled names or had poor handwriting, and indexers misread and mistyped names. Online digitized census sites may have updated their indexes or, in some cases, another researcher may have submitted a correction. Examine multiple census sites, including Ancestry.com, Archives.com, FamilySearch.org, findmypast.com, and HeritageQuest Online for different indexes and different quality images taken from different copies of microfilm.

We were able to locate Caroline after the death of her father in 1858 in the Villines household in both the 1860 and 1870 censuses. We further found Caroline's death certificate showing names of her parents, including Sophia's maiden name as Briggs. The couple's forenames could be seen in the 1850 census. The marriage bond further confirmed Sophia's maiden name, and it links William Whitefield and Dolphin Villines. The additional find of a marriage bond for Dolphin and Emily L. Briggs implies that the two women are sisters. That indicates that Dolphin and Emily Villines are Caroline's uncle and aunt. The presence of Caroline in the Villines household may indicate that Sophia is also deceased by 1860. We could continue our research to locate:

- A record of the death for Sophia D. Briggs Whitefield.
- Records of parents of Sophia and Emily, which may confirm that they were sisters.
- Guardianship records for Caroline and her other minor siblings between the date of death of her father and 1 June 1860, census day. Caroline's guardianship records may confirm that Emily is her aunt.

Summary

Each of the examples presented in this chapter involved a return to evidence that we had already obtained and a study of the details again. When you confront a brick wall, the lesson here is to reread each item thoroughly and question the content. This can help you focus on information that may previously have seemed of little consequence. The process also makes you focus on where the evidence was found and the quality of the contents, and compare multiple pieces of evidence. This type of detailed reexamination often brings to light new research possibilities—different document types, new repositories, new online websites and databases, and other resources.

The dissection of documentary evidence of all types is essential. Implied information can present new research paths. The death notice or obituary provides an excellent example of how to read between the lines to identify clues that point to specific information. You can then ask yourself what record types might contain that type of information, who might have created the record, where it would have been stored, and where it is today. Then you can seek to locate and access the original record or an exact image of it.

Chapter 2 continues with the use of what we call "brute force" in our research.

Sources Used in This Chapter

Cooper Cemetery (Caswell County, North Carolina). Grave marker.

Georgia, Atlanta. *The Atlanta Constitution*. 27 June 1918.

Martin, Virginia and Corinne. Photograph. ca. 1925. Privately held by Drew Smith, Tampa, Florida. 2013.

New Jersey, Essex County. 1900 U.S. federal census, population schedule.

New Jersey, Essex County, 1910 U.S. federal census, population schedule.

New Jersey, Essex County. 1920 U.S. federal census, population schedule.

New Jersey, Hudson County. 1930 U.S. federal census, population schedule.

New York, New York. Certification of Birth. Department of Health.

New York, New York. Soundex Index to Petitions for Naturalizations Filed in Federal, State, and Local Courts in New York City, 1792–1906 (M1674).

North Carolina. Application for marriage license.

North Carolina, Person County. 1860 U.S. federal census, population schedule.

North Carolina, Person County. 1860 U.S. federal census, slave schedule.

South Carolina. Division of Vital Statistics—State Board of Health. Standard Certificate of Death.

2

Use Brute Force

Standing in front of the brick wall in the deep forest, it probably occurs to you that you might be able to get past it by dislodging each and every brick, or by grabbing a sledgehammer and attacking the wall until it collapses from sheer human power.

In the context of genealogical research, we introduce this chapter with another common expression: "Leave no stone unturned." This proverb exhorts us to look for something by examining every possible location for its existence, not just the most likely or most convenient locations. Let's focus on convenience, for the moment.

Because we understandably want to make the best use of our limited time, we gravitate toward methods that appear to give us the information we need with the least amount of effort. We are thrilled that more and more documents are being scanned and put up online, because that means that we don't have to do the time-consuming and expensive work of traveling to the location of the document.

We appreciate when we encounter family history books with name indexes because that means that we don't have to examine every page for the names we're interested in. Why read an entire book if it has an index? You are probably guilty of jumping directly to a book's index rather than first referring to the table of contents, which may tell you that there are multiple books in the volume and multiple indexes. You may also skip reading the introduction, which may describe the index structure and important notations. In the interest of expediency, you may have missed clues that could have helped your research.

Why seek out original documents if they have been scanned and put up online? Digitized images of original documents make it possible to personally view and analyze the records ourselves. When the images are indexed, it is possible to quickly access them. Unfortunately, not every digitized document is every-name indexed, and that makes for a nearly insurmountable problem. As an example, a digitized last will and testament that is indexed only by the name of the testator doesn't reveal the other names included in the document. These may include the names of the heirs (and perhaps their spouses and children), the names of slaves left as bequests, names of nominated executors or administrators, and the names of witnesses. As a result, we lose important pointers to records of these other important people.

Not every original document has been microfilmed or digitized and, in the case of those that have been digitized, many documents may not yet have been indexed. We set aside, at least for the time being, the examination of databases of unindexed images, waiting until companies pay people to index them or until volunteer projects take on the challenge. Many genealogists don't realize that we used to have to use a manual approach with microfilmed records before images were digitized and placed online.

Why flip through page after page looking for an ancestor's name in an online archive of newspaper pages if the pages can be searched electronically? We're grateful when entire newspaper archives have been digitized and are full-text searchable, even though the Optical Character Recognition (OCR) indexing process is fraught with possibilities for errors.

It is important to remember that nobody is perfect and nothing is perfect. The person who indexed the book may have overlooked a name, or misspelled it. People responsible for indexing print or online documents may have misread handwriting. The person (or persons) responsible for digitizing a collection or original documents or print records may have missed a page. Mechanized systems that digitize microfilmed records may malfunction and skip an image or may produce an illegible image. And the software designed to turn a newspaper image into digital text may have encountered a fuzzy word that it couldn't read properly.

It is essentially your responsibility to consider all of these possibilities when you are looking for all the records that may relate to your ancestor. In order for you to better understand the drawbacks to using only these derivative documents, we'll review each type in detail.

Indexes

Any reader of non-fiction is likely to be familiar with the concept of an index because most non-fiction books have indexes in the back, making it easy to find all (or most) mentions of particular names, places, events, or concepts. A family history book that has no name index will likely elicit a groan and an uncharitable thought or two from a genealogist. In some cases, older family history and local history books that were originally published without an index are later reprinted with an added index, although not necessarily created by the original author.

Of course, if the book or set of records has no index, it doesn't mean that the researcher is allowed to ignore the resource. It means instead that the researcher will have to read the entire book or browse the entire collection of records.

Drew once taught a course to library science graduate students on the subject of indexing and abstracting. He was also hired to index a biography written by a faculty member at his university. So what was learned from these experiences?

First, indexing is as much an art as a science. The indexer must make countless decisions on what to include in the index and what to exclude. If someone other than the author of a book is doing the indexing, it can be even trickier. An indexer does not always know or understand the author's intent. For instance, the indexer might think that the author is referring to two different people when instead the author is just using variant names for the same person. As a result, there may be multiple entries in the index for the same individual. Or the indexer might confuse two different people as the same person, and index them that way. Indexed place names can suffer the same problem as a result of spelling variations or when a city and a county have the same name.

Second, an indexer might make other kinds of mistakes. One or several pages can be skipped accidentally. Or the indexer might misread a name and spell it differently in the index. Creating an excellent index is painstaking, tedious work, and the resulting index is unlikely to be considered perfect, even by the indexer.

So far, we've been talking about indexing typewritten books. If we now consider indexing of handwritten documents, the problems obviously multiply. It is far too easy to misread a handwritten name or place in a genealogical record, and an indexer may be predisposed to choose a name or place that is already familiar. This means that relatively unusual first names,

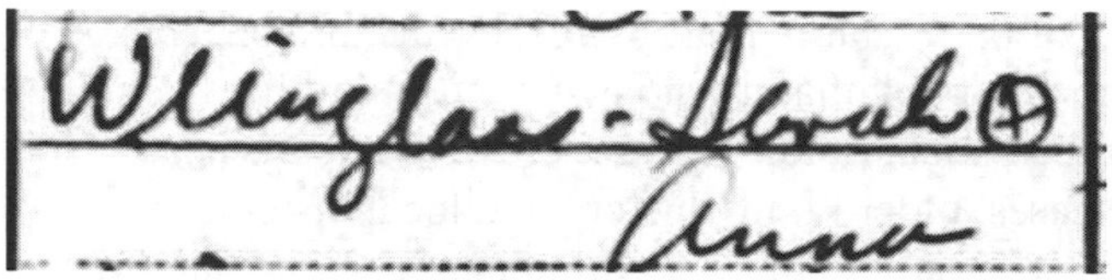

FIGURE 2-1 1940 U.S. federal census entry for Sarah Weinglass and Anna Weinglass (by permission of Ancestry.com)

last names, or geographic names may end up being misindexed as a similar, more common name. You may be aware that the indexing of some online databases provided by commercial services has been outsourced to countries where the residents are unfamiliar with the names and places listed in the records, resulting in numerous indexing errors.

Let's look at one instance. In Figure 2-1, Sarah Weinglass and her daughter, Anna, were enumerated at 3923 Laurel Avenue in Kings County, New York. The indexer misread the surname as Weinglan. In addition, the enumerator originally indicated the place as "New York City" in Kings County, New York. Someone subsequently lined through the city and wrote "Brooklyn." The indexer, however, entered New York. This also could cause a failed search if you specified in your search that they lived in Brooklyn, Kings County, New York. In this example of an online index, there are multiple errors that could frustrate your search. You would have to manually browse many pages of documents or use one or more of the search strategies described later in the chapter.

Fortunately, some online databases allow the addition of corrections or annotations when a user finds an error in an index entry. Ancestry.com and Fold3.com are examples of services that currently allow this.

Transcriptions

While the words "transcript" and "transcription" have many different meanings, such as those used in law or medicine, here we are concerned only with the idea of copying text, whether originally handwritten or typed. A transcription is supposed to be the creation of an *exact* copy of a document.

That means that it should include every character of the text and punctuation exactly as it appears. There should have been no attempt made to correct grammar, spelling, and punctuation. The intent is to preserve an exact copy of the document's content.

Genealogists frequently transcribe the contents of probate records, gravestones, or obituaries. Unfortunately, any instance of copying done by a human being is likely to involve interpretation, especially if the original source is handwritten. As a result, errors may be introduced into the final product. Even worse, the transcriber may go through multiple steps, such as handwriting a copy of the original source, and then typing the final product from his or her handwritten version, meaning that there are multiple opportunities to introduce errors.

Remember that a clerk was responsible for entering every handwritten document found in a county's marriage, will, and deed books, and other official records. That person was transcribing from another document, and he or she may have introduced errors into the transcription.

It is for these reasons that articles have been written and tutorials produced to educate genealogists on the best practices in transcribing documents, especially those that were originally handwritten. To help those researchers who may be working only from the transcript instead of from the original document, the transcriptionist is expected to be perfectly clear regarding placements of words and punctuation, and to identify places where the text is too difficult to read. This means that the researcher, who is likely to be more familiar than the transcriptionist with the family discussed in the document, might have success in interpreting difficult-to-read language in cases where the transcriptionist failed. FamilySearch.org executed one of the best indexing projects on the 1940 U.S. federal census records. Volunteers generated indexes of the census population schedules by transcribing information listed on these documents. These transcriptions were reviewed for accuracy. When two people disagreed on the handwriting, an arbitrator also reviewed the record and made the final decision about the correct interpretation.

James Alexander. Carpenter. New Minister, Cecil Co., Md. July 12, 1717. C. 103. Wife, Mary; youngest son, Ffrancis; sons, Joseph and John; another child, not named; father-in-law, John Steel, Yeoman, of New Castle Co.; brother, Ffrancis Alexander of Cecil Co., Md. Exc. wife, Mary; father-in-law, John Steel; brother Ffrancis Alexander.

FIGURE 2-2 Example of a printed abstract

Extracts

An extract is a specific selection of information from a source document (see Figure 2-2). It, too, is expected to preserve the exact spelling and punctuation of the original document. Unlike a transcript, however, an extract is created by intentionally discarding some information while preserving other information. For instance, an extractor might go through years of old newspapers, extracting the names of couples that were married and copying some of the text of the marriage announcements. A genealogist who is depending only upon such an extract might miss an important clue, such as the fact that the groom or bride was widowed at the time of the marriage. Extracts of antebellum deed books and wills, for example, may also omit the names, ages, and other information about slaves, thus stymieing the efforts of the African-American researcher to locate information about his or her ancestor.

Abstracts

An abstract is very similar to an extract in that the abstractor has made decisions as to what information to include and what to ignore. Abstractors seldom transcribe the text from the original document and may not preserve any of the spelling and punctuation. For genealogical purposes, a typical abstract will ignore legal boilerplate language, although even this can be tricky if the boilerplate language has been altered to provide potentially useful genealogical content (such as when the person making the will refers to him or herself as "being of sound mind but weak body"). It can be difficult to determine the criteria that the abstractor may have used to copy or ignore information, and the resulting abstract may be constructed in such a way as to confuse the significance of some of the statements in the original. Many abstracts contain only the briefest of information.

Another complication may result when a compiler combines his or her transcription, extract, or abstract with material gleaned from material other than the original source. *Wills of Richmond County, Virginia, 1699–1800* by Robert Kirk Headley (Genealogical Publishing Co., 1983) presents abstracts of wills but also substitutes information from Order Books, 1692–1699 to supplement wills and estate records prior to existing wills from 1699. This may extend the research possibilities, but the data was derived from sources with possibly different methods of recording details. Each type of record would need to be personally evaluated from a different point of focus.

It may seem easier to accept transcripts, extracts, and abstracts as sufficient proof of some fact, but nothing could be farther from the truth. Your personal examination of each original document is essential to ensure that you have all of the information for evaluation. Your personal familiarity with the person or family you are researching can provide a much better insight into the evidence you are reviewing.

OCR in Detail

Although it currently (and for the foreseeable future) requires a human being to reliably transcribe information from old handwritten records, information science has made great strides in designing software that can interpret typed documents, such as books and newspapers. The OCR process mentioned before has been successful in providing full-text indexing to print books or microfilmed or digitized newspapers.

If you have ever used an online database to search for a name in an old family history book or old newspaper, you have experienced the convenience of OCR. However, you may not have realized that you also experienced the problems. Despite the fact that the quality of the transformation from image to electronic text has improved greatly in the past few years, it is still the case that OCR software is not 100 percent accurate. In some cases, the error rates may be as high as nearly 30 percent, depending upon the quality of the source

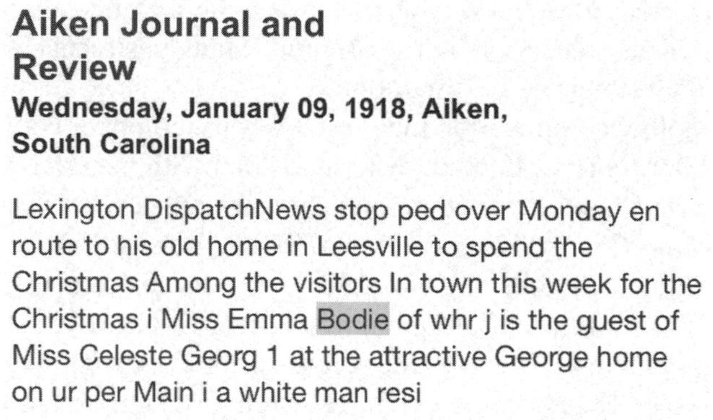

**Aiken Journal and
Review**
**Wednesday, January 09, 1918, Aiken,
South Carolina**

Lexington DispatchNews stop ped over Monday en
route to his old home in Leesville to spend the
Christmas Among the visitors In town this week for the
Christmas i Miss Emma Bodie of whr j is the guest of
Miss Celeste Georg 1 at the attractive George home
on ur per Main i a white man resi

FIGURE 2-3 OCR result for a
portion of a newspaper page

material being indexed. Other than the "intelligence" of the
software itself, the accuracy of its results depends on many
factors: the quality of the original image, the fonts used
in the original document, whether or not the image was
skewed when it was created, the layout of text in the original
document, the porosity of the paper used, the smearing of ink
on the original, and so forth. Newspapers present a special
challenge to OCR processing because of the way in which ink
tends to "bleed" on the cheap newsprint paper. As a result, it
can be difficult even for a human to read, let alone software.

Let's look at an example of poor OCR results for one
newspaper entry from the *Aiken Journal and Review* from
9 January 1918. Figure 2-3 shows the somewhat garbled result
of the OCR scan from the original newspaper page shown in
Figure 2-4. Broken letters in the printed text were omitted,
and hyphenated words were not properly recognized.

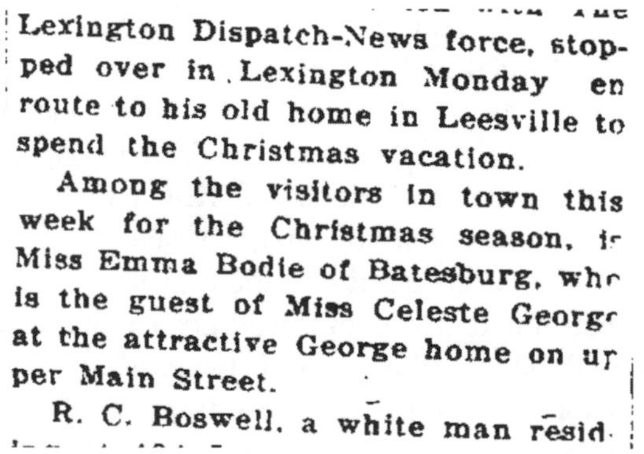

Lexington Dispatch-News force, stopped over in Lexington Monday   en
route to his old home in Leesville to
spend the Christmas vacation.
    Among the visitors In town this
week for the Christmas season, i-
Miss Emma Bodie of Batesburg, whr
is the guest of Miss Celeste Georg-
at the attractive George home on ur
per Main Street.
    R. C. Boswell, a white man resid-

FIGURE 2-4 The newspaper page
from which the OCR scan was
derived

Sources of Secondary Information

Up until now, we have been focused on derivative sources of information: indexes, human-created transcriptions, extracts, abstracts, and documents produced by OCR, which is essentially a form of machine-created transcription. Using these sources means that we are at least one step removed from the original sources.

Regardless of the type of source we are using, we face another pitfall in the analysis of the information itself. Even an original source can contain a mixture of information, some of which is considered to be more reliable because the information was compiled at the time of the relevant event, and some of which is more suspect because of the passage of time, which can result in faulty memories or the use of secondhand information.

Just as we can divide information sources into the categories of original and derivative, we can divide the information itself into the categories of primary and secondary. The birthdate provided on an original birth certificate is normally considered to be primary information, while the birthdate provided on a tombstone for an elderly person is normally considered to be secondary information.

The point here is not that primary information is always good or that secondary information is always bad. After all, it is entirely possible that no source of primary information exists, and in such cases, we must depend upon whatever secondary information is available, if any. Nor is it the point that primary information is always reliable. Nothing prevents someone from writing down an incorrect name, date, or place on an original record.

The point, then, is that genealogists sometimes content themselves with using secondary information in those cases where access to the secondary information is quick and easy, while access to the primary information is more time-consuming or expensive. Again, the brute force technique should be applied where simple or cheap research methods are insufficient to break through the brick wall.

Family Histories, Online Family Trees, and Personal Web Pages

The term "compiled genealogy" can be used to refer to any source of information where a researcher has produced genealogical information about a family. In pre-computer times, this may have been in the form of a published family history or of manuscript papers eventually donated to a library or archive. Today, we not only have digital access to many of these published family histories, but we also have countless online family trees. These trees may be found in both the online databases of major commercial and non-commercial genealogical services, but on privately maintained websites, perhaps discoverable by using a search engine.

Compiled genealogies are obviously a mixed bag. Some of the earliest ones were complete fabrications created for some political, social, or religious purpose. Later compilations that may have been commissioned by a wealthy or prominent individual may even have been tweaked by the hired researcher to give a result pleasing to the patron. Your great-aunt Lydia's written family history may have included fictitious details designed to enhance the family's reputation or to hide some unpleasant or unsavory information. Setting aside cases of nefarious motivation, compiled genealogies are still the product of individuals with varying levels of research skills, and who may or may not be detail-oriented.

Before you get the impression that we're telling you to ignore compiled genealogies, we want to point out that many published family histories and online family trees were created by intelligent and skilled genealogists who took great care in their research work. Ideally, they identified the sources that they used, and in many cases they reproduced images of those sources so that others could check their work.

The problem, of course, is that you're not likely to know from the beginning whether any particular compiled genealogy should be trusted, although seeing images of the source documents is a good sign. But the reality is that, when the compiled genealogy does not provide images of (or links to) the consulted documents, it falls to you to locate those documents yourself, so that you can ensure that the author of the compiled genealogy did not make errors of interpretation. This is more work, certainly, but it is probably the only way to get past the brick wall.

Application Forms to Societies and Other Organizations

Another group of documents that genealogists often refer to are applications completed by people wishing to join heritage, lineage, and other organizations. Some of these in the United States include the General Society of Mayflower Descendants, the Jamestowne Society, the Colonial Dames of America, the National Society of Colonial Dames, the National Society Daughters of the American Revolution, the National Society Sons of the American Revolution, the United Daughters of the Confederacy, the Sons of Confederate Veterans, the Sons of Union Veterans of the Civil War, the Society of the Cincinnati, and more. (Cyndi's List has links to many lineage organizations at http://www.cyndislist.com/societies/lineage.) Applicants must complete an application and supply documentation substantiating their descent from an ancestor who participated in a specific way in historical events.

Many states also sponsor pioneer descendant programs that seek to document a direct relationship to a pioneer ancestor. For example, the Florida State Genealogical Society's Florida Pioneer Descendants Certification Program honors descendants of individuals who settled in the Territory of Florida prior to Florida achieving statehood on 3 March 1845. Documentation of each generation going back to before the date of statehood is required for certification. This program also has a county-level certificate program that honors persons whose ancestors settled in an area before it became a county.

The applications for these organizations may be available for your review in a number of formats. It is important to remember that membership criteria may have changed over time. In addition, the review of applications and supporting documentation may become more stringent over time and require more evidence. Consider, for example, the Daughters of the American Revolution, which has published the *Patriot Index* in print form. It includes images of actual applications made by individuals. In reviewing some older applications, it is possible to identify errors or discrepancies missed in the application review process in decades past. The DAR has made available its Genealogical Research System (GRS), an online resource at http://services.dar.org/public/dar_research/ search designed to aid general genealogical research and to assist with the DAR membership process. The GRS is a collection of databases that provide access to the many materials amassed by the DAR since its founding in 1890. You can locate an application and order a copy online for review.

Other organizations may provide access to copies of the applications and documentation resources on microfilm, via photocopy services, or by another method.

The "Reasonably Exhaustive Search"

For many years, the Board for Certification of Genealogists (BCG) has promoted the concept of a "Genealogical Proof Standard," a set of guidelines for engaging in genealogical research such that the products of that research is of sufficient quality that the conclusions of that research should be accepted by those who encounter it. Specifically, the Genealogical Proof Standard consists of five elements, the first of which is a "reasonably exhaustive search." In other words, the genealogical researcher is expected to seek out the widest variety of genealogical records relevant to the time and place of the events being researched.

George's book *How to Do Everything: Genealogy* covers nearly two dozen of these possible source types, but that book is not meant to identify an exhaustive list of every kind of information source that a genealogist might find useful. Different geographic areas and time periods will require the researcher to seek out different kinds of records. If you do not already own genealogy guides for specific countries, states, or ethnic groups, this might be the time to seek them out from your local public library or from online booksellers. You can also find free online research guides published in the

FamilySearch Research Wiki at https://www.familysearch.org/
learn/wiki. In Chapter 5, we'll talk about using online forums
to discover previously unknown record collections for your
areas of interest. You will want to learn about the geographical
location and what records were created there at the time your
ancestor lived there, and then learn more about locating and
working with those types of records.

If identifying all possible record collections to be searched
is your first step, your second step is to locate these particular
collections. Recognize that some record collections may
still be stored at the courthouse or some other governmental
facility in the county in which they were created. They may
have been relocated elsewhere, however. For example:

- Land, property, and real estate tax records may have
  been accessioned to a state archive.

- Wills and estate papers may have been accessioned to a
  state archive.

- Birth records may have been transferred to a state vital
  records office, a department of vital statistics, or state
  health department. Copies may still be available at local
  or county vital records locations.

- Marriage records may have been accessioned to a state
  archive.

- Death records may have been transferred to a state vital
  records office, a department of vital statistics, or state
  health department. Copies may still be available at local
  or county vital records locations.

It also is possible that original records may have found
their way into the possession of local genealogical or
historical societies or into public or academic library special
collections. The Hillsborough County, Florida, marriage
records, consisting of the bride and groom indexes and the
original marriage licenses and certificates, were saved from
destruction and added to the University of South Florida
(USF) Tampa Library's Special Collection.

As this chapter has already suggested, don't content yourself
with locating only the index to a collection, especially if the

collection itself still exists. The third step is to familiarize yourself sufficiently with the collection so that you can plan an effective search. How is the collection organized? Is it chronological, alphabetical, or a mixture? If it's alphabetical, are the surnames alphabetized based on the entire surname or just the first letter of the name? What is the scope of the collection (time period, geography, and so on)? If there are columns, what does each column mean? What do the abbreviations mean? This may mean that you want to spend some time interacting with the custodian of the collection, such as a librarian or archivist, to obtain assistance and tips in conducting an effective search.

If the collection is searchable online, spend time with the help documents to see what your available options are. Are there special characters (wildcards) that you can use to represent problematic letters in your search, keeping in mind that you're looking for ways to get around errors made in indexing, transcription, or OCR processing?

Let's review a few tips for searching an online collection (when an exact search for the first and last name doesn't turn up any relevant results):

- Leave either the first name or last name fields blank, if possible. This will increase the chances of locating someone if the original recorder of information or the indexer botched the spelling of part of the name.

- If leaving the first or last names blank results in too many results, you can use other features of the index, such as date limits or geographic limits to reduce the number of results. But do this carefully so as not to miss an important record.

- If you are planning a search where you are leaving the first or last names blank, you can also use database options that may let you give first or last names for other family members. For instance, you can look for every John who had a daughter named Mary.

- Look at adjacent counties, especially if your ancestor lived near a county boundary. Look at adjacent states if your ancestor lived near a state boundary. Look in other countries if the boundaries changed over the time period that your ancestor lived there.

■ When searching databases based upon addresses, such as census records or city directories, search for neighbors if you know them from other records. For instance, if you found your ancestors in the 1920 census but can't find them in the 1930 census, look in the 1920 census for their neighbors and see if you can find those same neighbors in a later census. (We go into more detail about this technique in Chapter 3.)

■ If you are searching a database that isn't naturally divided into fields for such things as first and last names (for instance, newspaper databases or Google itself), use different arrangements of the names you are seeking. An exhaustive search for John Smith will require searching for "John Smith," "Smith John," "John ? Smith," "J Smith," and "Smith J," just to name some of the possibilities. Be sure to see what punctuation mark you should use to represent a missing middle initial, and be careful for those cases where an ancestor may have had multiple middle names.

■ Try alternate spellings for common names. For example, William may have been spelled as Will, Bill, or Wm. Try alternate spellings for surnames. An example might be Schmit, Schmitt, Schmidt, or Smitt. Also, learn to misspell the person's name in the event that others may have misspelled it.

■ Use wildcards if the online database offers that option. At Ancestry.com, for example, you can use an asterisk (*) to represent one or multiple letters in a name, or you can use a question mark (?) to substitute for a single letter. You can use these wildcard characters only when you specify the Exact Match search option on the search template. Check the Help facility at each online site to determine if wildcard search options are available, what they are, and how to effectively use them.

After you have used the search features of the online collection, if you still have not yet turned up any records that relate to your brick-wall ancestor, you may need to browse every document. While nobody will expect you to examine every page of a particular United States census looking for your family, a lot can be said for examining every page of a single Enumeration District (ED) where your family is likely to have lived. For example, the ED boundaries may have changed from one decennial census to another. ED maps have been microfilmed for the 1880 through 1940 censuses, and they are available for order through an LDS Family History Center. A comparison of ED maps for a specific area may reveal changes in the boundaries. Your every-page search through the correct ED may turn out to be the only way to discover a family member where either the enumerator or the indexer botched the spelling of the family name.

We also realize that the location of the original documents may make it infeasible to personally inspect them. In later chapters, we discuss using volunteers or professionals to help do that kind of work.

Needless to say, if you've given up on finding your ancestor in a book or database because you don't see them in the index, transcript, extract, or abstract, perhaps you should consider returning to that source and painstakingly viewing every page.

Example 1

A transcription of one man's will listed his children's names as "William, John, Isaac, Elizabeth, Mary Margaret and Jeanette." An examination of the actual will in the probate packet revealed that there was a comma between Mary and Margaret, thereby identifying that this was not one daughter but two.

When working with wills, it is essential to obtain a copy of the original document for your personal examination. Pay particular attention to the names of the witnesses, as they are frequently relatives. The name(s) of the nominated executor, executrix, or administrator is also important. That person may be a relative or a close friend. You will want to research each of these people to determine how they were related or associated with the deceased or the family.

The will is just the start. Other documents are generated during the probate process, and every document in the probate packet that was deemed significant enough for inclusion and should be carefully examined. Here are some of the most important documents, each of which may provide names and information that may extend your research.

- **Letters of Administration**   The probate court receives the will and seeks to prove that it is, in fact, the last will and testament executed by the deceased (the testator). The court then awards Letters of Administration to the executor(s) of the estate. These authorize the person(s) to transact all types of business on behalf of the estate. Make sure to obtain copies of all of the probate court minutes from the court records. These include every communication about and court action related to the estate. You may also encounter names of persons not otherwise listed in the estate papers.

- **List of potential heirs**   The first act of an administrator is to identify all of the potential heirs of the estate. These people may have been named in the will or referred to by relationship. "My son Edgar and his heirs forever" or "my grandson" are common statements. Inferred heirs, based on known or proven relationships, must also be identified. Once identified, each of the potential heirs must be researched, and each heir must be located. It is imperative to determine if a potential heir is living or deceased. If dead, his or her children may be entitled to inherit, depending on the terms of the will. Each heir must be contacted. The names and addresses of these heirs can extend your research reach in a number of additional directions.

- **Inventory of the estate**   The executor must determine the full extent of the estate and therefore an inventory is performed. Each asset is listed and values are assigned to each item. A review of the inventory can provide insight into the financial status of the individual, the occupation, the lifestyle, and more. The presence of books in an inventory may indicate that the person or someone in the household was literate. Look again at the will to determine if the deceased signed the actual will or if an "X" was used as the person's mark. (U.S. federal census population schedules from 1850 forward record whether a person could read and write.)

■ **Real estate information** The inventory should include references to any real estate owned or interests held jointly with another person, a bank, or another entity. These references should send you in search of real estate records, *and* you should look at both the grantor and grantee indexes for the county. Determine the individuals from whom the deceased purchased or inherited property or to whom he or she sold or gave property. Look at the witnesses' names and try to determine their relationship, if any, to the deceased.

■ **Public notices** The executor is required to publish one or more notices in a local newspaper to alert debtors and creditors of the deceased to contact him or her to settle outstanding debts. Copies of the notices may be included in the probate packet or they may be cited as handled in the probate court minutes. You may also want to locate those notices in historical newspapers.

■ **Documents related to settlements** Documents related to settlements of accounts with debtors and creditors may be included. These may provide clues to other aspects of the deceased's activities.

■ **Auction and sale records** The auction or private sale of assets of the estate may occur. The probate packet will include details about such sales of property, including the names of purchasers and the amounts of the sales. Family members may buy personal items and livestock at auctions that they want and that the heirs

are willing to liquidate. Research these persons and
determine their relationship to the deceased. Sons-in-
law can often be identified and married daughters who
may have "disappeared" can be found.

■ **Accounting records**   The executor is required to
account for every piece of the estate. Accounts payable
and receivable may be presented to the court for review at
various times during the probate process. They also are
summarized and a report submitted to the probate court,
typically on an annual basis There may be a single
report prior to the final settlement of an estate or reports
may be submitted for multiple years. Read the reports
and look for names that may imply personal or familial
relationships.

Each of these types of probate documentation may reveal
names, addresses, relationships, and other details that can fill
in gaps in your knowledge about the individual and the family.
Remember that the probate court minutes should never be
overlooked. Probate files may be missing from a courthouse
for a variety of reasons. The minute books, however, will
detail all the activity about the estate that was presented to
the court. These books are maintained and indexed for quick
access by the judge and the court personnel. They can now
provide ready access for your research, especially if they
provide information about lost or missing probate documents.

Example 2

When Drew began researching his family in the early 1990s,
he realized that some of his ancestral surnames would be
easier to research than others. His Smiths, Martins, and Kings,
who tended to have common first names, were relatively
difficult to make progress on, especially for a genealogical
beginner. But his great-grandmother's family name, Bodie,
looked more promising.

Fortunately, he was not the first person to do research into
the lineage of the Bodie family. One of the best published
genealogists of the early twentieth century was John Bennett

Boddie. Boddie had published a number of volumes about Southern U.S. families, including his own. Drew soon discovered a lot of background on the Boddie/Bodie family in John Bennett Boddie's *Seventeenth Century Isle of Wight County, Virginia*, originally published in 1938. Chapter XIX, "The Boddie-Bodie Family in South Carolina," carried the descendants of the original Boddie immigrant from Virginia through North Carolina into the Edgefield District of South Carolina, where Drew's great-grandmother Jane Bodie was from. In the book, John Bennett Boddie listed Jane herself and her first husband (Drew is descended from Jane's second husband), together with Jane's siblings and parents.

Unfortunately, John Bennett Boddie identified very few sources for his work. Boddie had listed Jane and twelve siblings, including sisters Mary, Ann, Manda, Elizabeth, Amorilla, Susan, Virginia, and Jennie. But as Drew began to look at census records, some things didn't add up. Boddie appeared to have missed the youngest daughter, Emma, who had died young. Setting aside the omitted Emma for the moment, was Boddie correct in saying that there were nine daughters?

Drew had begun his serious work on his family history after his favorite aunt had passed away in 1992. That aunt was affectionately known as Aunt Jenny (sometimes spelled "Ginny"), but Drew knew that her real name was Virginia. So did Jane Bodie have a sister named "Virginia" and another named "Jennie"? Boddie had said that Virginia was born in 1848 and that Jennie was married to a man with the surname of "Riley," but Drew's research led him to conclude that Virginia and Jennie were the same woman, and that Virginia was married to Burr Hampton Riley. Boddie had turned one woman into two different women, perhaps by using multiple sources and not making the connection of the nickname to the real forename.

To be completely fair, we cannot rule out the possibility that a Virginia was born in 1848, died early, and then another child born in 1850 was given the same name. But that explanation wouldn't completely exonerate Boddie because of another error he made. Drew found the idea of a daughter being named "Amorilla" in 1839 in South Carolina to be farfetched. The 1850 U.S. federal census (the earliest census in which individuals are named beyond the head of household) showed only seven women in the country with that name, none of whom were in the South. Could Boddie have looked at a census and misread the handwriting of the enumerator?

Boddie had provided birth years for Jane and a number of her siblings, and those dates matched calculated birth years based upon the ages of the children in the 1850 census. This strongly suggested that Boddie had gotten his birth years from the 1850 census. If Amorilla had been born in 1839, we could expect to find her as an 11-year-old in the 1850 census, but the census showed a daughter of that age with the name of Amanda. Boddie had said that Jane had a sister named Manda, who had married Willis Holmes. Later censuses showed that Willis Holmes had a wife named Amanda.

When Drew looked at Amanda's name in the 1850 census, he suddenly realized that the handwritten name could have been misinterpreted as "Amorilla," meaning that Manda and Amorilla were one and the same person, Amanda. (See Figure 2-5.)

If Drew had never examined the likely source documents and had depended only upon a published family history, he would have perpetuated the errors surrounding Jane Bodie's siblings.

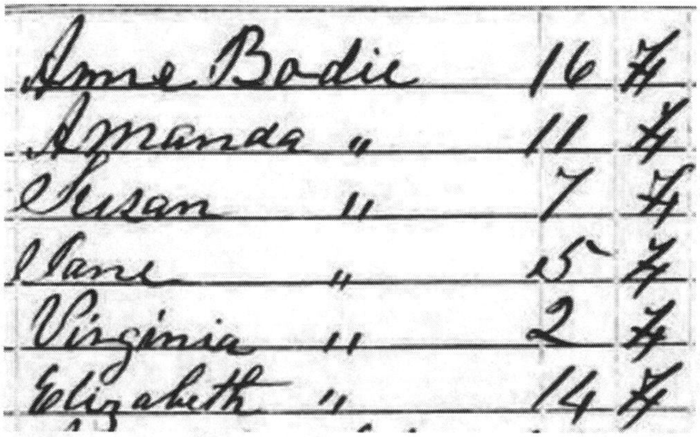

FIGURE 2-5 1850 U.S. federal census, Edgefield District, South Carolina (by permission of Ancestry.com)

Example 3

One of George's long-standing brick walls involved tries to trace the first husband of his grandmother. Minnie Wilson of Mecklenburg County, North Carolina married Jeter Earnest Murphy on 2 February 1898. She recorded the event in her personal Bible. He unfortunately died on 9 July 1898 of typhoid fever. Minnie also recorded Jeter's death. George was interested in learning more about Jeter's origins. He searched online databases of HeritageQuest Online, Ancestry.com, and findmypast.com with no results. His breakthrough came when he visited the Family History Library in Salt Lake City, Utah, and located the microfilmed record of the granting of Letters of Administration for Jeter Murphy's estate, filed in Iredell County on 23 January 1899. That document names "Wm. Murphy and sister Miss Murphy" as entitled heirs to the estate (see Figure 2-6).

FIGURE 2-6 Completed Letters of Administration application for the estate of Jeter Murphy, 23 January 1899

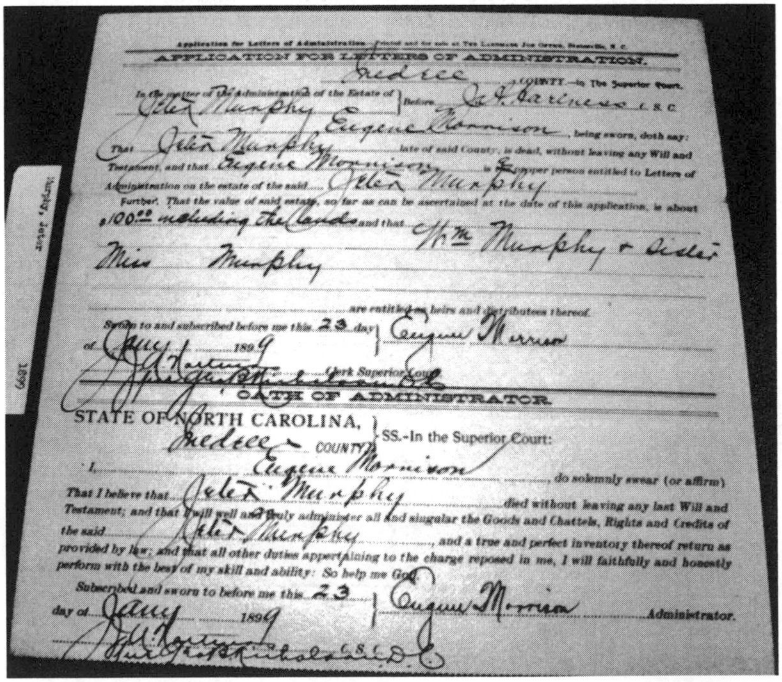

APPLICATION FOR LETTERS OF ADMINISTRATION.

Iredell COUNTY.—In The Superior Court.

In the matter of the Administration of the Estate of Jeter Murphy — Before J. A. Hartness C.S.C.

Eugene Morrison, being sworn, doth say: That Jeter Murphy late of said County, is dead, without leaving any Will and Testament, and that Eugene Morrison is the proper person entitled to Letters of Administration on the estate of the said Jeter Murphy.

Further, That the value of said estate, so far as can be ascertained at the date of this application, is about $100.00 including the lands and that Wm Murphy & sister Miss Murphy

are entitled as heirs and distributees thereof.

Sworn to and subscribed before me this 23 day of Jany 1899 — Eugene Morrison

J. A. Hartness, Clerk Superior Court

OATH OF ADMINISTRATOR.

STATE OF NORTH CAROLINA, Iredell COUNTY, SS.-In the Superior Court:

I, Eugene Morrison, do solemnly swear (or affirm) That I believe that Jeter Murphy died without leaving any last Will and Testament; and that I will well and truly administer all and singular the Goods and Chattels, Rights and Credits of the said Jeter Murphy, and a true and perfect inventory thereof return as provided by law; and that all other duties appertaining to the charge reposed in me, I will faithfully and honestly perform with the best of my skill and ability: So help me God.

Subscribed and sworn to before me this 23 day of Jany 1899 — Eugene Morrison, Administrator.

J. A. Hartness C.S.C.

View Record	Name	Parent or spouse names	Home in 1880 (City, County, State)	Birth Year	Birthplace	Relation to Head of House	View Image
Matches 1-1 of 1 Sorted By Relevance							
View Record ★★★★★	Willie Murphy	Mary	Bethany, Iredell, North Carolina	abt 1875	North Carolina	Grandson	📄

Results per page: [50 ⁝]   1-1 of 1

Figure 2-7 Search result for Willie Murphy (by permission of Ancestry.com)

Armed with this information, George returned to the 1880 census indexes at Ancestry.com and searched for William Murphy in North Carolina. He found no matches. However, he used a wildcard search in the 1880 census at Ancestry.com for Wil* Murphy. The asterisk is a wildcard that, as mentioned before, represents one or more letters. The search was successful, yielding a match to a record for Willie Murphy in Bethany, Iredell County, North Carolina (see Figure 2-7).

The list of other household members living together includes a brother (Peter) and a sister named Lessie (see Figure 2-8) living with their mother, Mary Murphy, in the home of Mary's parents, Bluford and Elizabeth Cooper.

Figure 2-8 List of all household members living with Willie Murphy in 1880 (by permission of Ancestry.com)

Bluford Cooper	71
Elizabeth Cooper	59
Elija Cooper	20
Mary Murphy	33
Lessie Murphy	10
Peter Murphy	7
Willie Murphy	5
Fannie Colbert	17
George Obrien	30

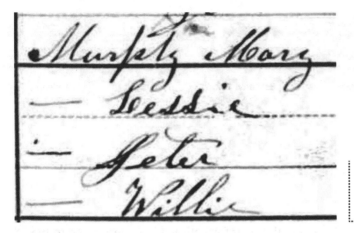

FIGURE 2-9 Detail from an 1880 U.S. federal census image showing Jeter Murphy (by permission of Ancestry.com)

Examination of the actual census document (see Figure 2-9) shows the middle of the three children to be Jeter Murphy. The *J* was indexed as a *P*. New searches for Peter Murphy in Ancestry.com, FamilySearch.org, and findmypast.com all found matches for Peter Murphy. Ancestry.com allowed George to enter a recommended correction.

As a result of this work, George was able to successfully locate Jeter Murphy as a seven-year-old child in 1880 with his mother and siblings, and was able to also identify his maternal grandparents. Had he not located the probate record, he probably would never have linked to another member of Jeter's family and therefore successfully located the three generations living together. This breakthrough allowed George to also find newspaper articles and an obituary at NewspaperArchive.com, and a cemetery stone photograph in the Oakwood Cemetery in Statesville, North Carolina, at Find A Grave (memorial #63676039).

Summary

Some parts of genealogical research are relatively easy, but brick walls usually require extra effort. Derivative sources, including indexes, transcriptions, extracts, and abstracts, can introduce errors or omit important information, suggesting that a look at the original sources may provide the clue that identifies the brick-wall ancestor. It may be easy to trust a published family history, online tree, or personal website, but you should always use such sources as pointers to the more reliable information, and not as the endpoint of your research.

BCG's Genealogical Proof Standard includes the idea that serious researchers engage in a "reasonably exhaustive search." This involves seeking out all known and available records relevant to the place and time of your ancestor's life events. Once the records have been identified and located, the researcher will need to take special care in examining the records, not only by using careful search strategies, but also by browsing every document page where feasible and appropriate.

In both the previous chapter and this chapter, we have focused primarily on solving a research problem by specifically looking for records mentioning a brick-wall ancestor. In Chapter 3, we'll get a bit sneakier and figure out how to do an indirect assault on that brick wall.

Sources Used in This Chapter

Ancestry.com.

Historical Research Committee of the Colonial Dames of Delaware, abstr. and comp. *A Calendar of Delaware Wills, New Castle County, 1682–1800*. New York: Frederick H. Hitchcock, 1911.

FamilySearch.org

Findmypast.com

NewspaperArchive.com.

New York, Kings County. 1940 U.S. census, population schedule.

North Carolina, Iredell County. Application for Letters of Administration.

North Carolina, Iredell County. 1880 U.S. census, population schedule.

South Carolina, Aiken. *Aiken Journal and Review*. 9 January 1918.

South Carolina, Edgefield District. 1850 U.S. census, population schedule.

3

Go Around the Wall

In the previous two chapters, we explored two very different research techniques for getting past a genealogical brick wall: one that resembles using a magnifying glass and a set of tweezers, and another that is more like using a battering ram. Both techniques require hard work and can often result in some success, but neither technique would strike the beginning genealogist as especially clever.

Again, envision yourself in the dense forest, facing that tall, wide, imposing wall. What if you're going about this the wrong way? Could the solution for getting past the wall involve nothing more than walking around one of the ends of the wall, or backtracking to a fork in the forest path and seeing if the other path forward leads to a detour around the original brick wall?

When you are dealing with brick walls, it is easy to become locked into thinking only about your brick wall ancestors or their immediate families. This tunnel vision can cause you to miss a valuable genealogical research technique. For this chapter, English writer John Donne's famous line, "No man is an island," will help you remember a valuable research technique. With rare exceptions, all human beings throughout history have spent their lives as part of a broader human society. As a researcher, you can take advantage of that social interconnection to find a less direct route to learn more about your brick wall ancestors.

You may have already realized that you might find out more about your ancestor if you spend some time researching their spouse(s), their parents, or their children. After all, these are people with whom the ancestor would have spent a lot of time, and whose records may mention the ancestor of interest. But why stop with those particular individuals? What about siblings, aunts, uncles, cousins, in-laws, and other relatives? For several years, George has used the phrase "sidestep genealogy" to refer to researching all of these family members, and many of us may have used this technique without even being aware of it.

The Broader Technique (and What to Call It)

If all you did at this point was to move your focus from a particular ancestor to their near and far relatives, you would likely make much more progress than you would make if you ignored the other individuals, but you would still be barely scratching the surface of possibilities for research leads. If you think about all of the people you spend significant time with in your own life today, you would likely think about your friends, your neighbors, your co-workers, people you buy goods and services from, people who are members of the same organizations that you are, and so forth. The same list was certainly true for our ancestors. Research all of these people and you may learn something about your ancestor.

Before we move forward, we think it's helpful to provide a name for the research technique that we're going to describe in detail and provide examples of. Although the technique has been written about and taught for decades, it may not have had any kind of real name until at least the early 1990s when the phrase "cluster genealogy" or "cluster research" first appeared in print, and was further popularized by genealogy writer Emily Anne Croom beginning in the mid-1990s. A few years later, noted genealogist Elizabeth Shown Mills adopted a memorable and useful acronym to help her students remember the key components of this technique, namely, the "FAN Club," which stood for "family, associates, and neighbors." Mills began to use this term in presentations at national genealogy conferences, and under this name the technique has become much better known to the genealogical community.

Note   If you look online for references to this technique, you will find that many of them use the "F" in "FAN" to stand for "friends" instead of "family," but we prefer the "family" version because friends are arguably a type of associate and we don't want to forget the extended family as we do this type of research.

Spouses

To get you accustomed to this technique, we'll start at the center of the circle of people surrounding your ancestor of interest. Because our married ancestors may have shared their lives for many decades (the longest-known marriage was one that lasted more than 91 years!), we should not be surprised that they will show up together in numerous records. Even after one spouse has died, there may be obituaries, probate records, real estate and property records, and gravestones that continue to tie the two individuals together. If you have had difficulty in finding records based on the name of your brick-wall ancestor, search instead for records naming the spouse(s), including:

- Census records and city directories
- Birth records
- Marriage records
- Church records
- Military records (including pension records)
- Newspaper stories (including advertising notices)
- Letters, postcards, diaries, and family Bibles
- Property records, probate records, or other legal records that may mention the names of spouses
- Immigration records, such as ships' passenger lists, because spouses may have traveled together
- Family, local, and church histories that mention a spouse and/or the extended family
- For instance, someone may have written a family history for the spouse's family, and mentioned to whom the spouse was married.
- Photographs
- Death records, obituaries, gravestones, and other burial-related records

As you learn more about the spouse(s), you may discover clues about the target ancestor. For instance, the geographic location of the first spouse prior to the marriage may suggest where the target ancestor was living. When you are struggling to identify the maiden name of a female target ancestor, look at the neighbors of the husband's family prior to the marriage. They may point you in the right direction. More about neighbors later.

Parents and Children

Parents and children, like spouses, may have closely connected lives for many decades. Not only will the children usually be with their parents before the children reach adulthood, but older parents may also be living with one or more of their adult children in later years, especially if the parent has been widowed. Children who never marry may stay with their parents throughout their lives or, at the very least, live nearby. For all of these reasons and more, you should research your target ancestor's known parents and children. The following list identifies key documents where someone is likely to be listed with a parent or child:

- Census records
- Marriage records (these may mention the parents of the marrying couple)
- Church records, especially baptismal and christening records, and church histories
- Military records (including pension records). Children sometimes apply to obtain a pension based on the service of a parent.
- Letters, postcards, diaries, and family Bibles
- Property records, probate records, or other legal records that may mention the names of parents and children.
- Immigration records, such as ships' passenger lists, since parents and children may have traveled together
- Naturalization records, specifically United States naturalization records between 10 February 1855 and 31 December 1921, a time period during which derivative naturalization was granted for wives and minor children of alien men
- Family and local histories
- Photographs
- Death records, obituaries, gravestones, and other burial-related records. For instance, Drew's paternal grandfather is listed on the same gravestone as his grandfather's parents and grandmother (Drew's great-grandparents and great-great-grandmother).

It may seem daunting, especially if your brick-wall ancestor had a large number of children, but researching each child (not just your direct ancestor) in detail may provide clues or inferrences to new information. That may include identifying where your ancestor was living in later years or where he or she died or was buried. Your "missing ancestor" may have been buried in the cemetery lot with his or her child and in-laws.

By now, you should be getting the idea that almost all common types of genealogical sources should be searched, not just for the names of the ancestor of interest but also for the names of their spouses, parents, and children. From this point forward, we won't repeat the same lists of sources. However, we will highlight some records that you should be looking for.

Other Relatives

As you move away from spouses, parents, and children, the circle gets bigger, and the number of people to research increases. Even so, these other individuals are likely to have had contact with and been included in documented interactions with your ancestor, and should not be ignored:

- Siblings (including half-siblings)
- Grandparents and grandchildren
- Aunts, uncles, and cousins
- In-laws
- Step-relatives

Beyond the "F"

If you have exhausted looking at the family members, both close and extended, of your brick-wall ancestor, it's time for you to move to the rest of the club. With whom, other than family, did your ancestor associate? Who are all the people who qualify as the "A" and the "N" in the FAN Club?

Prior to the post–World War II mobility of modern society, your ancestors frequently stayed in one place for many years, if not for their entire lives. Even when they migrated from one country to another or from one part of a country to another part, they often relocated in groups. For instance, it would not be unusual to find a group of people from a small town in Europe migrating together to the same place in North America. In North America, it was not unusual for people from one ethnic or religious group to relocate as a group to another location for a variety of reasons. Beginning in 1755, the British expelled the Acadians who had settled in Nova Scotia, New Brunswick, and Prince Edward Island, and they migrated to other places, including Maine and Louisiana. A group of George's direct ancestors, the Alexanders of Cecil County, Maryland, were Scots-Irish Presbyterians. Several of the Alexander brothers and a significant number of their neighbors in the same Presbyterian congregation wanted to acquire land and resettle together. Those families, along with their minister, migrated in the 1740s around the top of the Chesapeake Bay and south to settle in Mecklenburg County, North Carolina.

In rural areas, the same families may have surrounded your ancestors for generations, and in urban areas, your ancestors' neighbors may have belonged to the same ethnic groups or religious organizations, and had similar occupations.

Your ancestors may have intermarried with neighbors. This means that researching the neighbors may eventually turn out to be researching your ancestor's extended family, except that you may not know yet how they are related. There are a number of sources you can use to determine the neighbors of your ancestor, including city directories, property maps, tax lists, and censuses. Figures 3-1, 3-2, and 3-3 illustrate three people with the same surname living close to one another on Chambers Street in Newark, New Jersey, according to an 1893 city directory. This should suggest that you should research each of them to determine if and how they are related.

Smith Mary A, Mrs, glassbending, 65, h 85 Chambers

FIGURE 3-1 City directory entry for Mary A. Smith

FIGURE 3-2 City directory entry for Patrick Smith

Smith Patrick, glassbender, h 82 Chambers

FIGURE 3-3 City directory entry for Philip Smith

Smith Philip, glassbender, h 80 Chambers

Whether or not your ancestor's neighbors intermarried with your family, the neighbors still had an impact on the life of your ancestor. They may have:

- Witnessed your ancestor's legal documents
- Bought and sold property in a transaction with your ancestor (or your ancestor's estate)
- Appeared in a newspaper story with your ancestor (for example, as guests at a wedding or other social event)
- Attended the same church or other religious institution as your ancestor
- Attended the same school as your ancestor
- Enlisted in the same military unit as your ancestor
- Mentioned your ancestor in a letter, diary, or journal (or they may have been mentioned by *your* ancestor in a letter, diary, or journal)
- Become involved in a lawsuit with your ancestor (on the same or opposite sides)
- Been buried in the same cemetery as your ancestor
- Been a pallbearer at your ancestor's funeral (or your ancestor may have been a pallbearer at theirs)

While many of your ancestor's associates were neighbors, obviously not all were. They may have simply shared the same place of employment, religious institution, school, military unit, or commercial interest. Or they may have been neighbors in the past, and yet they kept in touch when one or the other moved.

Another Important Use of the FAN Club Technique

One of the dilemmas facing genealogical researchers is when it is unclear whether two different references in the genealogical records are referring to one individual or two. The fact that both references are to people with the same name doesn't mean that they are the same person. Some names are very common, after all. And just because the references are to people with two different names doesn't necessarily mean that these are two different people. After all, our ancestors often chose to use different names at different times in their lives, or their names were occasionally misrecorded in the records. In the previous chapter, you saw an example where a researcher took two slightly different references to Amanda Bodie and incorrectly concluded that the references were to two different women (and he probably made the same mistake for her sister Virginia). How can the FAN Club technique help in preventing these kinds of errors?

Because individuals have their own unique networks of family, associates, and neighbors, we would expect some, if not many, of those same people to show up in different references to the same individual of interest. Imagine that you've got references to individuals from two different sources, and the individuals have the same or very similar names. Let's refer to the individual mentioned in the first reference as "Candidate 1" and the individual mentioned in the other reference as "Candidate 2." We want to know whether Candidates 1 and 2 are the same person or two different people. If we can't find any overlap between the FAN Club of Candidate 1 and the FAN Club of Candidate 2, that should raise a red flag. On the other hand, if we find a great deal of overlap, that should give us some confidence that we are dealing with the same individual.

This method still has some drawbacks. Close relatives, who may have nearly identical FAN Clubs, may share the same first name (fathers and sons, mothers and daughters). First cousins, who may be close to the same age and have much the same social network, may also share the same name.

A name originally given to a deceased child might be reused for another child a year or two later. However, if you can rule out these exceptions, you can use the FAN Club technique to make a significant amount of progress in determining whether you have found a record referring to your ancestor or are faced, instead, with another person of the same name.

Other Names

Scrutinize all of the documents related to a family for alternate names. It was not unusual for a man to be referred to using his initials rather his name. One of George's ancestors, Joseph McKnitt Wilson, for example, was often listed in documents and indexes, and often in newspapers, as J. M. Wilson or as Jos. M. Wilson.

Married women's names can cause confusion in your research. Women whose husbands were living were addressed as and referred to as Mrs. and their husband's name. After the husband's death, a woman may have been addressed as Mrs., her own first name, and her husband's surname. For example, Mrs. Sylvanus Minton, as a widow, became Mrs. Caroline Minton. This situation can be compounded if she was also generally known by a diminutive of her first name or a nickname, as was this same woman when her name appeared in her sister's obituary as "Mrs. Cal Minton of Alabama."

In some cases, too, a person may never have used his or her given name. George's paternal grandmother was named Laura Augusta Wilson, but she was always known as Minnie. (Minnie was the name of her mother's best friend and the child was called Minnie in honor of the friend.) In fact, every official document, from censuses to marriage records to death certificate and cemetery marker, all list her name as Minnie.

Nicknames may also confound your research if they were used instead of the real given name. You may find clues to nicknames in family correspondence and other non-official documents. You will then need to relate the nickname to the correct individual in the family, sometimes using documents such as letters and school records rather than legal documents. Genealogy database software packages typically accommodate entry of a nickname or alternate name so that you are reminded of it every time you access the record. We urge you to make use of this field in your database so that you don't lose sight of a nickname's use.

These types of name variations, even beyond intentional spelling changes and spelling errors, can present brick walls in your research. Focus on being flexible in your searches in records, regardless of whether you are browsing physical indexes or using a computer to search for records. Be alert to the potential spelling variations, spelling errors, *and* the use of alternate names or nicknames, and be certain to look at every possibility.

Example 1

Imagine that you were looking for Drew's half-great-uncle, Michael Luther Long, who was born in December 1873. By 1880, his father, Wiley Long, had died, and his mother, Jane Bodie, had remarried to Drew's great-grandfather, Edmon[d] M. Martin. But Mike Long was not with his mother and stepfather in the 1880 U.S. census. Where else could you look? Jane's stepmother, Nancy Bodie (and therefore, Mike's step-grandmother), was still alive in 1880 and living in the same county as Jane and her new husband. If you look for Nancy in the 1880 census, shown in Figure 3-4, you find Nancy, her own children, her stepchildren, and 6-year-old "grandson" Mike Long in the same household.

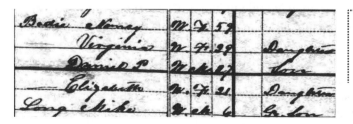

FIGURE 3-4 1880 U.S. federal census for the household of Nancy Bodie, including step-grandson Mike Long (by permission of Ancestry.com)

Example 2

Drew's grandmother, Rachel Weinglass, was the daughter of Louis and Sarah Weinglass. Hoping to learn Sarah's maiden name, Drew sent for Rachel's SS-5, the form she completed when she applied for a Social Security account number. (See Figure 3-5.) (By this time in her life, Rachel Weinglass had married a Catholic named William Henry Smith and had taken the first name of Elizabeth as part of her religious conversion.) In the field that asks for the "mother's full maiden name," Rachel provided "Sarah Weinglass." While it would not be impossible for both Louis and Sarah to have had the same last name prior to marriage, Drew figured that it was far more likely either that his grandmother did not know her mother's maiden name, or that she had misread the instructions.

Drew realized that he could obtain the SS-5 for one of Rachel's siblings. He chose to obtain one for Rachel's oldest sibling, her brother Jack. In Jack's SS-5, shown in Figure 3-6, Jack indicated that his mother's full maiden name was Sarah Grodowitz.

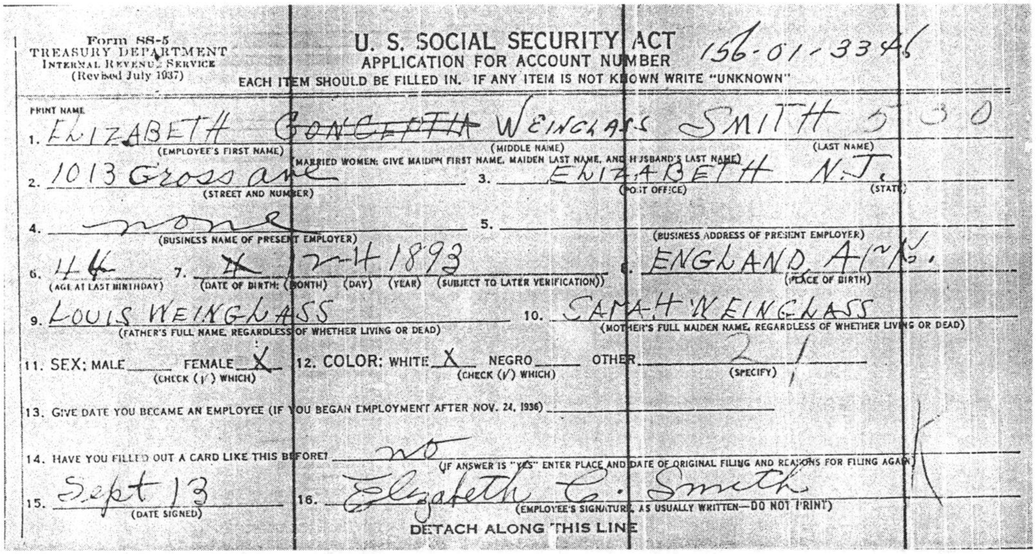
Form SS-5
TREASURY DEPARTMENT
INTERNAL REVENUE SERVICE
(Revised July 1937)

U. S. SOCIAL SECURITY ACT
APPLICATION FOR ACCOUNT NUMBER 156-01-3346
EACH ITEM SHOULD BE FILLED IN. IF ANY ITEM IS NOT KNOWN WRITE "UNKNOWN"

PRINT NAME
1. ELIZABETH ~~CONCEPTA~~ WEINGLASS SMITH
(EMPLOYEE'S FIRST NAME) (MIDDLE NAME) (LAST NAME)
(MARRIED WOMEN: GIVE MAIDEN FIRST NAME, MAIDEN LAST NAME, AND HUSBAND'S LAST NAME)

2. 1013 Gross ave (STREET AND NUMBER) 3. ELIZABETH N.J. (POST OFFICE) (STATE)

4. none (BUSINESS NAME OF PRESENT EMPLOYER) 5. (BUSINESS ADDRESS OF PRESENT EMPLOYER)

6. 44 (AGE AT LAST BIRTHDAY) 7. 12-4 1893 (DATE OF BIRTH: (MONTH) (DAY) (YEAR) (SUBJECT TO LATER VERIFICATION)) 8. ENGLAND (PLACE OF BIRTH)

9. LOUIS WEINGLASS (FATHER'S FULL NAME, REGARDLESS OF WHETHER LIVING OR DEAD) 10. SARAH WEINGLASS (MOTHER'S FULL MAIDEN NAME, REGARDLESS OF WHETHER LIVING OR DEAD)

11. SEX: MALE ___ FEMALE X (CHECK (✓) WHICH) 12. COLOR: WHITE X NEGRO ___ OTHER ___ (CHECK (✓) WHICH) (SPECIFY)

13. GIVE DATE YOU BECAME AN EMPLOYEE (IF YOU BEGAN EMPLOYMENT AFTER NOV. 24, 1936)

14. HAVE YOU FILLED OUT A CARD LIKE THIS BEFORE? no (IF ANSWER IS "YES" ENTER PLACE AND DATE OF ORIGINAL FILING AND REASONS FOR FILING AGAIN)

15. Sept 13 (DATE SIGNED) 16. Elizabeth C. Smith (EMPLOYEE'S SIGNATURE, AS USUALLY WRITTEN—DO NOT PRINT)

DETACH ALONG THIS LINE

Figure 3-5 The SS-5 for Rachel Weinglass (aka Elizabeth C. Smith)

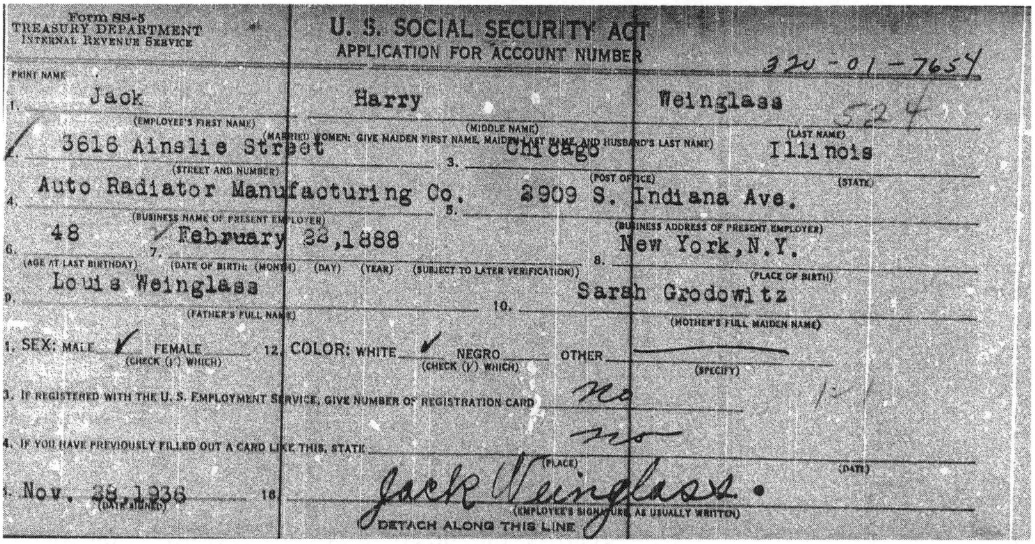

Form SS-5
TREASURY DEPARTMENT
INTERNAL REVENUE SERVICE

U. S. SOCIAL SECURITY ACT
APPLICATION FOR ACCOUNT NUMBER 320-01-7654

PRINT NAME
1. Jack (EMPLOYEE'S FIRST NAME) Harry (MIDDLE NAME) (MARRIED WOMEN: GIVE MAIDEN FIRST NAME, MAIDEN LAST NAME AND HUSBAND'S LAST NAME) Weinglass (LAST NAME) 524

2. 3616 Ainslie Street (STREET AND NUMBER) 3. Chicago (POST OFFICE) Illinois (STATE)

4. Auto Radiator Manufacturing Co. (BUSINESS NAME OF PRESENT EMPLOYER) 5. 2909 S. Indiana Ave. (BUSINESS ADDRESS OF PRESENT EMPLOYER)

6. 48 (AGE AT LAST BIRTHDAY) 7. February 22,1888 (DATE OF BIRTH: (MONTH) (DAY) (YEAR) (SUBJECT TO LATER VERIFICATION)) 8. New York,N.Y. (PLACE OF BIRTH)

9. Louis Weinglass (FATHER'S FULL NAME) 10. Sarah Grodowitz (MOTHER'S FULL MAIDEN NAME)

11. SEX: MALE ✓ FEMALE (CHECK (✓) WHICH) 12. COLOR: WHITE ✓ NEGRO (CHECK (✓) WHICH) OTHER (SPECIFY)

13. IF REGISTERED WITH THE U. S. EMPLOYMENT SERVICE, GIVE NUMBER OF REGISTRATION CARD no

14. IF YOU HAVE PREVIOUSLY FILLED OUT A CARD LIKE THIS, STATE no (PLACE) (DATE)

15. Nov. 28,1936 (DATE SIGNED) 16. Jack Weinglass (EMPLOYEE'S SIGNATURE AS USUALLY WRITTEN)

DETACH ALONG THIS LINE

FIGURE 3-6 The SS-5 for Jack Harry Weinglass

This discovery provided another surname for research into immigration, naturalization, and other record types.

Example 3

While researching the Tampa-based Milton family for a genealogy video series, we wondered if there were any living relatives for the family. The mother, Gennie, and daughter, Gloria Christine, were killed in an automobile-train accident in Tampa in April 1940. The father, Jesse Milton, died a few years later in Arizona, and the son, Charles, did not appear to have had any children. Drew focused on the more distant relatives to learn more about the family. The newspaper story of the tragic accident that had killed Gennie and Christine indicated that Gennie had picked up Christine on a Sunday morning at the home of an uncle, E. L. Milton. Additional research identified this uncle as Jesse Milton's brother, Elzie Lee Milton, who had a daughter, Betty, approximately the same age as Christine.

Was Betty still alive? The problem was that there was no easy way of knowing whether Betty had married and, if she had, whom she had married. Continued research about the life of Elzie Lee Milton indicated that he had married a second time, and had several additional children. By researching those children, half-siblings to Betty, Drew turned up a 1995 obituary for one of them that contained the name of a married half-sister whose first name was Betty. At the time of the research, Betty was still alive and living in Tampa, and she could be located. Drew used current Hillsborough County, Florida, online property records to locate Betty and her husband, and he also checked the SSDI for any record of either one's death.

Example 4

We often lose track of people from one census to the next. This can be complicated when you want to research siblings and collateral lines, but it can be important to locate and investigate the records of their lives when researching our direct ancestors. George experienced this situation when researching the siblings of his paternal grandmother, Laura Augusta "Minnie" Wilson. You first learned heard about her in Example 3 in Chapter 2.

Minnie was the youngest of nine children of Joseph McKnitt Wilson and Lydia Lenora Patterson Wilson of Mecklenburg County, North Carolina. Eight of the children reached adulthood and all of those children married. Tracing the marriages of these people was relatively simple using the records of Mecklenburg County.

George traced the locations where these people lived through the decades of their lives. He was aided by the fact that Minnie lived until 17 December 1966. From the time she and her husband, Samuel Goodloe Morgan, moved to Madison, Rockingham County, North Carolina in 1936, Minnie kept every Christmas card she had ever received in paper bags labeled by year and stored in the floor of her closet. All of these cards were in their original envelopes and the return addresses proved to be a bonanza for determining the residences of Minnie's siblings and their families through the years. These were a treasure trove for George's research.

The exception was her brother, Joseph "Joe" Patterson Wilson. There were no cards from him and his wife, Frances Lamb Mims Wilson. George found them together for the first time in the 1910 U.S. federal census in Columbia, Richland County, South Carolina. Joe was 40 years old and a hotel proprietor. Frances was 25, and the census indicated that the couple had been married for one year. (See Figure 3-7 for a photograph of the couple.) A search for Joe in the 1920 census yielded nothing. What had happened to the family?

George concentrated on Frances and found her in the 1920 census in Columbia, Richland County, South Carolina. She was listed as the head of household and was a widow, this time with four children: Joseph P. Wilson, Jr. (age 8),

FIGURE 3-7 Joseph Patterson Wilson and Frances Lamb Mims Wilson (from the collection of George G. Morgan)

George A. Wilson (age 7), Sarah E. Wilson (age 4 9/12), and William M. Wilson (age 2 6/12). Census day in 1920 was January 1. William's age suggests that he was born in the last half of 1917, also implying that his father must still have been alive as least into late 1916 or early 1917.

George had two questions he wanted to answer. First, when did Joseph Patterson Wilson die and where? Second, what happened to his wife and children?

George began with a search of America's GenealogyBank for Joseph P. Wilson. The first search result was an article in the *Charlotte Observer* (Charlotte, North Carolina) on 22 December 1916, page 11. The story is titled "Hotel Manager Meets Death in Bad Auto Wreck" and describes a collision between Wilson's car and a mule-driven wagon. Frances sustained a small scratch, and her children and one of Joseph's sisters, Mrs. R. C. Knox, riding in the back seat of the touring car, were uninjured. The article contains full details of the accident, the names of his surviving family members, and the plans for his funeral scheduled in Columbia, South Carolina, on 23 December 1916.

The search now resumed for Frances and her children. George searched the 1930 United States federal census at Ancestry.com for Frances Wilson without success. He next searched for daughter Sarah Wilson. He narrowed the search to specify a female, born in South Carolina, with the approximate year of birth of 1915 (+/– 1 year). The search results included a Sarah Wilson living in Miami, Dade County, Florida, as a stepdaughter of the head of household, George W. Thomas, married to Frances W. Thomas. (Figure 3-8 shows

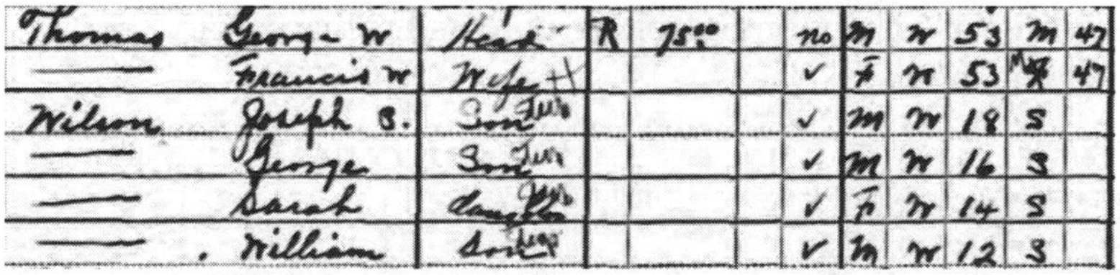

Thomas	George W	Head	R	75.00		no	M	W	53	M	47
—	Francis W	Wife H				✓	F	W	53	M	47
Wilson	Joseph B.	Son				✓	M	W	18	S	
—	George	Son				✓	M	W	16	S	
—	Sarah	daughter				✓	F	W	14	S	
—	William	Son				✓	M	W	12	S	

FIGURE 3-8 The 1930 United States federal census for Miami, Dade County, Florida located Frances with a new husband and her four children. (By permission of Ancestry.com)

details from the 1930 United States federal census.) Sure enough, there was Frances, and the couple had been married for about 6 years. Joseph P. Wilson (age 18), George Wilson (age 16), Sarah (age 14), and William (age 12) were all listed as stepchildren. The 1940 U.S. federal census found George W. Thomas and wife, Frances, living alone. However, the search was not over.

Florida conducted a number of state censuses between 1867 and 1945, and it was important to also check the 1935 and 1945 censuses. The family group seen in the 1930 federal census was still together in Dade County, Florida in 1935, as shown in Figure 3-9. The 1945 census told a different story. George W. Thomas and Frances W. Thomas were still living at the same address as in 1935. Living with them, however, were three people: Joseph P. Wilson, age 35, whose occupation was listed as army; Frances Wilson, age 8 and born in North Carolina; and Daphne Wilson, age 7 and born in Florida. This suggested that Joseph P. Wilson had married and produced two daughters.

A search of Florida Marriage Records at FamilySearch.org quickly located the image of a marriage license application dated 4 July 1935 in Fort Lauderdale, Broward County, Florida, for Joseph P. Wilson and Mary Frances King (see Figure 3-10).

A search of the U.S. World War II Army Enlistment Records, 1938–1946, database at Ancestry.com provided a record for Joseph P. Wilson, born in South Carolina and living in Dade County, Florida (see Figure 3-11). He enlisted on 5 August 1942 at Camp Blanding, Florida. He had had four years of high school and worked as a general office clerk. Interestingly, he listed his marital status as divorced with no dependents. This was interesting information requiring an additional search for a divorce record and perhaps a custody settlement.

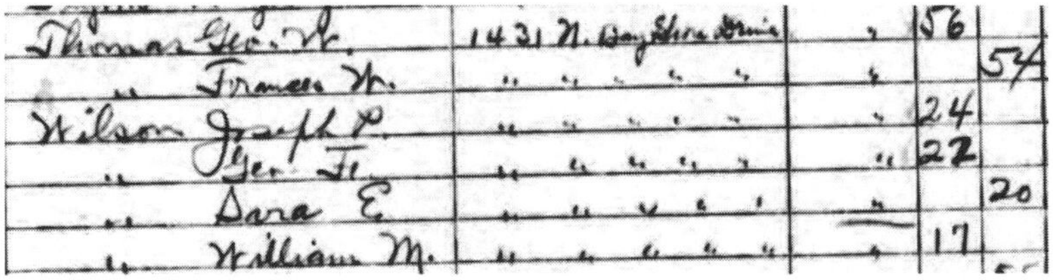

FIGURE 3-9 The 1935 Florida state census showing the family group in Miami, Dade County, Florida (by permission of Ancestry.com)

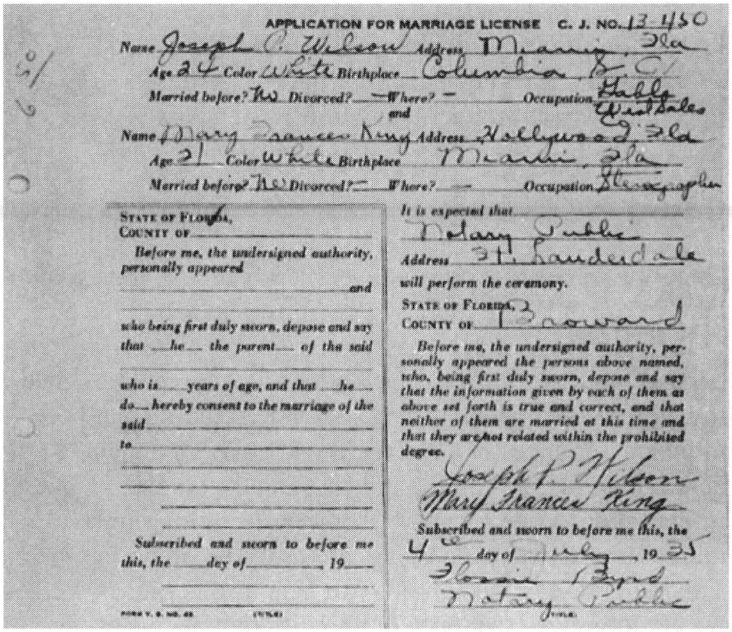
APPLICATION FOR MARRIAGE LICENSE C. J. NO. 13 450

Name Joseph P. Wilson Address Miami, Fla
Age 24 Color White Birthplace Columbia, S. C.
Married before? No Divorced? — Where? — Occupation Hobby Wholesale

and

Name Mary Frances King Address Hollywood, Fla
Age 21 Color White Birthplace Miami, Fla
Married before? No Divorced? — Where? — Occupation Stenographer

STATE OF FLORIDA,
COUNTY OF

Before me, the undersigned authority, personally appeared ______ and ______ who being first duly sworn, depose and say that ___he___ the parent___ of the said ______ who is ___ years of age, and that ___he___ do___ hereby consent to the marriage of the said ______ to ______

Subscribed and sworn to before me this, the ___ day of ______, 19___

It is expected that Notary Public
Address Ft. Lauderdale
will perform the ceremony.

STATE OF FLORIDA,
COUNTY OF Broward

Before me, the undersigned authority, personally appeared the persons above named, who, being first duly sworn, depose and say that the information given by each of them as above set forth is true and correct, and that neither of them are married at this time and that they are not related within the prohibited degree.

Joseph P. Wilson
Mary Frances King

Subscribed and sworn to before me this, the 4th day of July, 1935
Flossie Byrd
Notary Public

FIGURE 3-10 Marriage license application for Joseph P. Wilson and Mary Frances King

ancestry.com

U.S. World War II Army Enlistment Records, 1938-1946

Name:	**Joseph P Wilson**
Birth Year:	1911
Race:	White, citizen (White)
Nativity State or Country:	South Carolina
State of Residence:	Florida
County or City:	Dade
Enlistment Date:	5 Aug 1942
Enlistment State:	Florida
Enlistment City:	Camp Blanding
Branch:	Branch Immaterial - Warrant Officers, USA
Branch Code:	Branch Immaterial - Warrant Officers, USA
Grade:	Private
Grade Code:	Private
Term of Enlistment:	Enlistment for the duration of the War or other emergency, plus six months, subject to the discretion of the President or otherwise according to law
Component:	Army of the United States - includes the following: Voluntary enlistments effective December 8, 1941 and thereafter; One year enlistments of National Guardsman whose State enlistment expires while in the Federal Service; Officers appointed in the Army of
Source:	Civil Life
Education:	4 years of high school
Civil Occupation:	Clerks, general office
Marital Status:	Divorced, without dependents
Height:	70
Weight:	139

FIGURE 3-11 Record for Joseph P. Wilson from the U.S. World War II Army Enlistment Records, 1938–1946, database (by permission of Ancestry.com)

    George had successfully answered his two questions and, by conducting "a reasonably exhaustive search," had revealed additional clues and evidence to continue the research of this line to locate and contact living family members.

Summary

Once we realize that our ancestors left behind evidence of their lives not just in their own records, but also in the records of their family members, associates, and neighbors, we can expand our research focus beyond a single target individual to a much larger group of people. Understanding the ways in which our ancestors interacted with others can help us determine the kinds of records we should examine. Although researching a large group of people instead of a single individual may seem daunting, the rewards can be significant. This same research technique can help us determine whether we are looking at evidence of two different people or of only one. What makes our ancestors unique is not just the individual actions they took throughout their lives, but also the social circle that surrounded them, whether by choice or circumstance. One extremely valuable benefit of this research technique is the broadening of our perspective of the geographical, historical, *and* social contexts in which our ancestors and their families lived. We learn how they were affected by all of these influences and how they participated in their communities.

Sources Used in This Chapter

Florida, Broward County. Application for Marriage License.

Florida, Dade County. 1930 U.S. census, population schedule.

Florida, Dade County. 1945 state census, population schedule.

Holbrook's Newark City and Business Directory and Full Co-Partnership Directory, Official for the Year Ending May 1, 1893. Newark, New Jersey: Press of the Holbrook Printing Company, 1892.

National Archives and Records Administration. *U.S. World War II Army Enlistment Records, 1938–1946* [database online]. Provo, Utah: Ancestry.com Operations Inc., 2005.

Social Security Administration. Applications for Account Numbers, Form SS-5. Social Security Administration, Baltimore, Maryland.

South Carolina, Edgefield County. 1880 U.S. census, population schedule.

Wilson, Joseph Patterson and Frances Lamb Mims. Photograph. Privately held by George G. Morgan, Tampa, Florida. 2013.

4

Talk to a Friend

If you've ever watched the popular TV show *Who Wants to Be a Millionaire?*, you may recall that contestants are given a number of "lifelines," which are different ways to get help when answering the questions. One of these lifelines (no longer an option) was known as "Phone-a-Friend," and it enabled the contestant to call a friend or family member who was knowledgeable in the area needed to answer the question.

Sharing your problem with someone else can sometimes help demolish your genealogical brick walls. Later in the book, we go into some detail about the advantages and disadvantages of hiring a genealogical professional researcher to get past brick walls. In this chapter, however, we discuss options that don't involve costs or contracts.

Why Share a Brick Wall Problem?

When you first encounter a brick wall problem, you may begin with a lot of assumptions about what you already know to be true. This is as a result of your own personal knowledge of specific record types, and experience with working in specific venues, as well as your expertise with using online resources. As time goes by, you may eliminate certain research paths because you have judged them to be unproductive at some point or in some way. Your long-term exposure to your brick wall problem may mean that you're now wearing psychological blinders. It really is possible that you may have become too close to your problem, unable to step back and give it a fresh view.

But a fresh view can be provided by someone else who is not already familiar with the problem. They are unlikely to have all of the same assumptions about what is already known or about which research methods have been exhausted. Their emotional detachment from the problem means that they won't be shy about pointing out areas that you have overlooked or shortcuts that you may have taken. Like the child at the end of "The Emperor's New Clothes," another individual may be able to give you an honest appraisal of your situation that you have become unable or unwilling to see.

With Whom Should You Share the Problem?

Your first thought might be that you should share your brick wall with another genealogist, and that is certainly an option that we'll discuss shortly. Before you take that direction, however, you might consider talking about the problem with the non-genealogists among your family and friends. Even genealogists can be guilty of having some assumptions about the way in which research can and should be done, but non-genealogists aren't burdened by such ideas. As you describe your brick wall problem to a non-genealogist, you certainly may find yourself having to explain in more detail what kinds of records you've looked at and how you've gone about your research. You will need to describe what information you are seeking and why you chose specific record types. As you engage in this process of explaining exactly what you are doing, why you are doing it, and what you have or have not yet learned, you'll be putting yourself in the mindset of someone who is new to research and to the resources you have used. You are very likely to find that this process of explaining will expose gaps in what you have done and will trigger ideas as to new research paths to take. For example, you might realize that living descendants of the individual or other relatives may have documents, a family Bible, or other materials that might extend your research.

Now, let's assume that you're going to share your research problem with a fellow genealogist. This could be someone who is a member (close or distant) of your own family, a member of one of your genealogy societies, or someone you've exchanged information with online. In this kind of sharing, you're less likely to have to provide nearly as much detail as to the process of research you've engaged in, or what the record sources are all about. The other person is already going to understand what kind of information is available in a typical census record or marriage record. However, unless the person is closely related to you, they are not as likely to know much about the family you're researching, and their questions to you will guide your story and ensure that you haven't left anything important out. Unlike sharing with a non-genealogist, you may find that sharing with another genealogist will sensitize you to those areas of your research where you took shortcuts or made assumptions about what you had learned, or it will bring to light records and places you may not have previously considered.

For example, let's say that you have been searching for a death certificate for your great-grandfather who died in North Carolina in 1910, and you have had no success. Another genealogist might suggest that you recheck the date on which the State of North Carolina passed legislation requiring the creation of birth and death certificates. You determine that the law was passed on 10 March 1913, and full compliance by all counties was not required by the state until 1920. As a result, the other genealogist might suggest that you look for alternate record types that might provide the date of death. These might include a probate record for his estate, a deed conveying ownership to property to an heir, a church membership roll entry, a newspaper obituary, or some other record that might document the date of death.

Because other genealogists are likely to have brick walls of their own, you might want to suggest that you trade stories, helping each other out. In fact, you might go so far as to actually offer to trade the two research problems so that you attempt to solve the other genealogist's research problem while they try to solve yours. Working on a new problem goes a long way to reducing your frustration levels. Each of you may also be able to advance the research of the other.

Finally, there is one other important group of listeners to share your brick wall with: librarians and archivists. As you work in libraries, archives, and other record repositories, you can use the opportunity to run your problem past the professionals and volunteers who staff the facility. Their knowledge of available local resources may give you new ideas for further research. They are likely to know of unusual or unique materials that you were unaware of, and they may be able to refer you to individuals or organizations who can provide suggestions.

How to Share a Brick Wall Problem

In *Alice in Wonderland*, the White Rabbit, about to relate a story, asks the King where to begin, and the King replies, "Begin at the beginning, and go on till you come to the end: then stop." Knowing how to begin telling your brick wall problem to someone else can be tricky because you don't want to bore or distract them with unnecessary information, but you also don't want to leave anything out that might turn out to be important to the solution.

Certainly, you're going to want to give the problem an appropriate context, identifying the relevant time period and geographic area, because this information is critical to identifying what kinds of records should be available. Next, you're going to want to identify exactly what your research problem is (identifying the names of parents, spouses, siblings, or children; identifying where someone emigrated from or immigrated to; identifying when and where someone was born, was married, died, or was buried; and so forth).

Then, you're going to need to identify what is already known, and how it is known (what sources were found and how they were found, where they were found, what information was or was not in the sources, and what the process was to form conclusions based upon the evidence provided by the information in the sources). You will need to describe your analysis and the hypotheses you reached. Finally, you're also going to need to explain what steps you have taken to solve the research problem, including what sources you have consulted and what process you used to consult them, and whether there are any sources that you have not yet consulted in relation to the problem and if so, why not.

During the process of sharing your brick wall problem, avoid rushing through the presentation. You will want to leave plenty of time for the other person to understand what they are hearing and to ask questions at each step. This will prevent you from accidentally glossing over something that you may have assumed to be true but that your listener will catch as a potential problem (or a new clue or research process to be followed).

As suggested earlier, the very act of sharing your brick wall problem with another person will cause you to slow down to rethink and verbalize the work you have already done. However, don't just stop at that point to go off to work on an idea you've stumbled upon. Make notes to yourself and continue the explanation. (After all, the idea you came up with might not pan out, and you don't want to have to start all over again later.)

If it's practical, don't merely tell your story to the other person. Show them images of the sources you have looked at, point to the information in the sources, and give the other person time to review the image and ask you questions about it. Your conversation will stimulate the thought process to recognize other possibilities and/or devise new research strategies.

In some cases, you won't be able to share your brick wall problem with another person either face-to-face or on the phone. You may want to prepare a type of published genealogical report. Professional genealogists create detailed reports for their clients and, in this situation, you are acting as your own client. If you need some inspiration as to how to write up your own brick wall problem, you might want to look at a genealogical journal that publishes case studies and similar articles. For instance, issues of the *National Genealogical Society Quarterly,* likely to be available in any large public library's genealogical collection, provide excellent examples of research problems described in written format. As you document your own problem, you can use published articles to suggest the structure and amount of detail you would want to provide anyone willing to examine your problem. Remember that the data you have entered into your genealogy database program, including source citations, media images, and notes, can typically be printed in reports to help you document your findings to date. An ancestor profile or timeline can also be used to document your research.

Let's look at some examples of the concepts we have discussed in this chapter.

Example 1

When Drew first became seriously interested in his family history in 1992, he found his great-grandmother Jane Belle Bodie especially interesting. Jane was married three times, and had children with her first two husbands. Drew's great-grandfather was Jane's second husband. Jane's third husband had the surname of Farmer, but Drew had no idea exactly where Jane Farmer was buried, although he reasonably supposed that it was probably in Laurens County, South Carolina, where the Farmers had lived.

The local genealogy society in Laurens County, the Laurens District Chapter of the South Carolina Genealogical Society, had produced a cemetery survey volume (*Burying Grounds, Graveyards, and Cemeteries, Laurens County, S.C.*) in 1990, but Jane Farmer was not listed in it. Drew then asked his mother where she believed her maternal grandmother to be buried, and her response was that Jane Farmer was buried in the "Old Laurens Cemetery." But no cemetery with that name appeared on any map.

Drew then traveled to Laurens to visit the local public library, and spoke with the librarian most knowledgeable about genealogy. When he asked her if she knew of any cemetery in Laurens County known as the "Old Laurens Cemetery," she responded that she did not, but that there was an Old Laurens *Mill* Cemetery, also known as the Northview Cemetery. This cemetery, which had not been surveyed in time for the first volume of the cemetery book, would be listed in the next volume (which was eventually published in 1998). The librarian said that she was assisting with the cemetery survey as a volunteer, and that she was one of the volunteers who had surveyed the Northview Cemetery. She had handwritten notes for that next volume in her office within the library, and she offered to bring them out for Drew to see. As soon as she did, Drew quickly found his great-grandmother listed, and the librarian said that because Jane's name was in the librarian's own handwriting, she could identify which row Jane was buried in (because she knew which rows she herself had surveyed).

The librarian went on to give Drew directions to the cemetery and, in less than an hour, Drew was standing at the grave of his great-grandmother.

Example 2

Libraries and archives do not always catalog the manuscript materials in their collections as well as you might like. These documents may, however, contain information that could help demolish the very brick wall you have encountered. You should recognize that creating catalog records is an expensive administrative process, and libraries and archives do not always have the funds to achieve the depth of cataloging that they might like to provide. However, you should never hesitate to make contact with the reference librarians at the facility to clarify their holdings and to request copies of materials.

Some collections, such as letters, diaries, and loose papers, may only be cataloged using some descriptive text. Others may include an inventory list of the contents of a group of materials. These inventories may list the names of authors or correspondents, or they may also include the names as keywords in the catalog for ease of location. Others may also include more details about the collection or of specific items, and may record dates and locations.

Journals and diaries are seldom catalogued by more than the name of the author and perhaps the beginning and ending dates of the work. Loose letters and papers are rarely cataloged with content details unless they were written by or concern an historically or socially important person. Individual sheet maps may also not be cataloged, depending on the repository.

The following are some excellent resources for identifying manuscript collections held by libraries and archives:

- **Access to Archives (A2)**   http://www.nationalarchives.gov.uk/a2a/ (part of the U.K. archives network)
- **ArchiveGrid**   http://www.archivegrid.org
- **National Union Catalog of Manuscript Collections (NUCMC)**   http://www.loc.gov/coll/nucmc/ (part of the Library of Congress)
- **WorldCat**   http://www.worldcat.org

Manuscript collections may contain a wealth of unique information that can help you to research around brick walls.

The reference staffs at the libraries and archives that house these collections are well trained to assist you in locating and accessing the contents. Feel free to make contact in person, by telephone, and by electronic communications.

There are other locations that should not be ignored. State libraries and archives, and many university libraries, have undertaken projects to identify, locate, and make many historical materials available to the public. These include digitized newspapers and photographs, vintage postcards, prints, sound recordings, film, and other resources. Be sure to keep an open mind about what different types of materials might have been created and that may now be available in a wide variety of formats. Be sure to ask genealogical and historical societies, as well as libraries and archives, about what items are available to you in a geographical area. Specifically ask if there are items that are not listed at their websites or in their searchable online catalogs. Vertical files containing clippings, letters, and other paper materials may exist with an extensive variety of materials. You may find your brick wall answer in any of these places.

Example 3

Genealogical societies and historical societies are excellent resources for helping you work around research roadblocks. They play important roles in their geographic area. These include: the preservation of local history and the promotion of local records conservation; the cataloging and recording of information about people and events in the community; fostering education about the history of the area and its people; and helping researchers access and use information.

These societies often work with libraries and archives to accomplish their goals. However, you will almost always find one or more society members who are exceptionally knowledgeable and who are happy to answer questions and provide guidance. The local public library reference staff may also be able to help.

You should make personal contact with a society to let the members know that you need some advice or assistance. Formulate your questions and communicate them. Ask if there are people who have knowledge of the history of the area and/or of the family you are researching. Request an appointment to speak with the person(s) one-on-one to discuss your problem. Here are some of the things that we have experienced:

- The society may have conducted one or more projects and created records that have not been published. These have included: cemetery transcription projects; indexes for newspaper obituaries; creation of newspaper subject clipping files (by name, location, and subject); collection and indexing of historical postcards, photographs, and stereographs; collection of funeral home books; and compilation of members' family group sheets.

- One or more society members may be longtime residents of the area and have personal knowledge of people, places, and events. Here are several examples:

  - A woman in Gainesville, Alachua County, Florida, was an authority on local history and created captions for almost every historical photograph and vintage postcard in the county library system's possession.

  - A chance encounter with a local resident in Edgefield County, South Carolina, led Drew and his brother to the tiny, isolated cemetery in which their great-grandmother's brother, the Rev. Jesse Pitts Bodie, was buried. (Years later, Drew learned that the local resident was an officer of the local genealogical society.)

  - A librarian working in the Heritage Room of the Rome-Floyd County Library in Rome, Georgia, had detailed knowledge of the contents of the George Magruder Battey, Jr., personal papers in the library's possession. Mr. Battey was the local historian for many decades. The librarian quickly located correspondence from the files between Mr. Battey and several of George G. Morgan's Holder family members. She also provided clipping files about the businesses dealings of his great grandfather, Green Berry Holder, in Rome, and written accounts concerning Mr. Holder's elections to the Georgia House of Representatives. In addition, she provided access to some of the original records of the United Confederate Veterans Camp Number 368 in the library's possession. She connected George with the administrator of the county school system who provided access to original local newspapers that had not yet been microfilmed. For the following several days, she offered contacts to other people in the area and, in subsequent years, has provided copies of a number of records and recommendations for other resources in the area.

Summary

Explaining your brick wall problem to another person can provide the fresh look needed to find a solution. Just the process of laying out the problem can generate new ideas, even when you are speaking with a non-genealogist family member or friend. But when your listener is another genealogist, a librarian, or an archivist, their unique skills may also lead to original and helpful suggestions.

5

Use Crowdsourcing

Human beings are a social species. Not only do we enjoy communicating with each other about our problems, but also we find that we can often solve problems in groups that we cannot solve alone. If a group of people was traveling together in the dense forest and came upon a brick wall, they could collaborate to invent new solutions that they could not have come up with if each one was traveling alone. For instance, the group could form a human pyramid that would allow someone to scale the wall.

The same is certainly true of genealogy. The brick wall problems that we all face are often difficult for us personally, but may be child's play for another genealogist. And when many genealogists work together to solve a puzzle, each may contribute an idea or work off the idea of someone else to carve a path forward.

So where will you find a group of genealogists? Let's look at your options.

Genealogy Societies

Long before there was an Internet, there were genealogy societies. For instance, the New England Historic Genealogical Society (NEHGS) has been around since 1845, and today, there are many hundreds of genealogy societies in the United States, Canada, the United Kingdom, Australia, New Zealand, and many other countries around the world. Nearly all of these societies have very similar objectives. They help to educate their members in how to engage in successful genealogical research, and they help to preserve and make available the genealogical records of their geographic areas. Many publish journals and newsletters, and maintain blogs or other kinds of websites. If they represent a small geographical area, such as a U.S. or English county, they may hold monthly meetings for their local members. In addition to their regular meetings and educational programs, they may have special interest groups that facilitate members coming together to discuss narrower genealogical topics, such as technology, DNA, or specific geographic or ethnic research. A few even have a special interest group (SIG) dedicated specifically to helping members with their brick walls.

If you are not already involved with a genealogical society, you should give serious consideration to joining at least two: one close to where you live, so that you can attend its meetings; and one or more distant societies that are located in the places where your ancestors lived. To find a genealogical society in the United States, use the website of the Federation of Genealogical Societies (FGS), located at http://www .fgs.org, and search its Society Hall (http://www.fgs.org/ cstm_societyHall.php), shown in Figure 5-1. FGS has several hundred genealogical societies, historical societies, and family

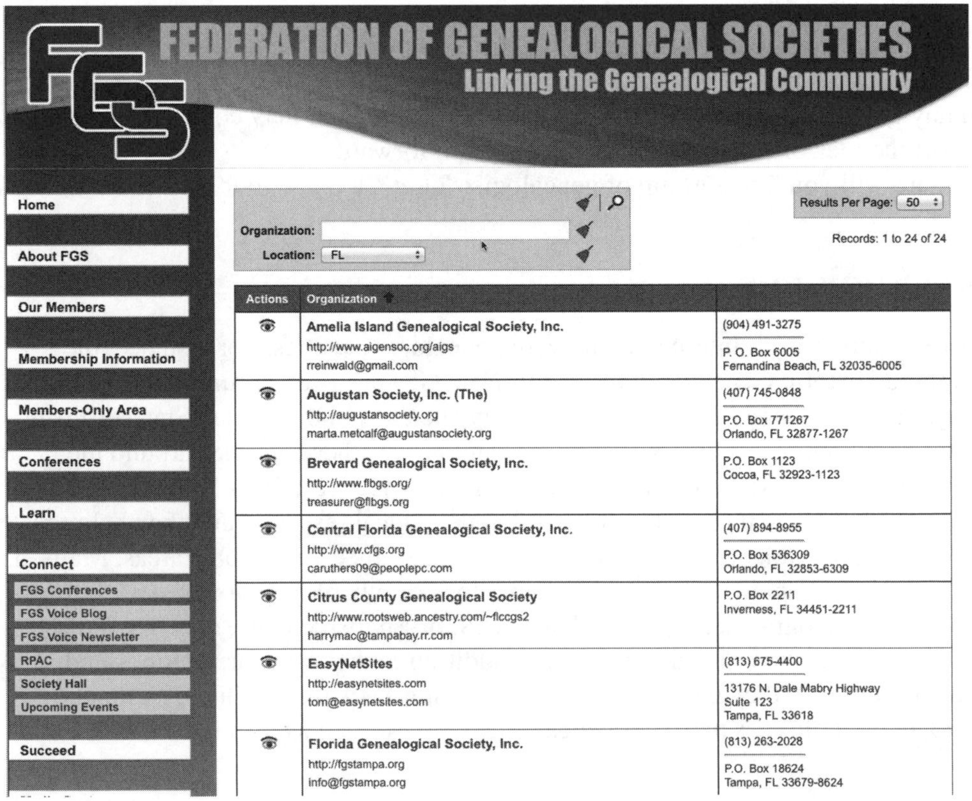

FIGURE 5-1 Federation of Genealogical Societies' Society Hall

associations as members. To locate a genealogical society in England, Wales, or Ireland, use the website of the Federation of Family History Societies (FFHS), located at http://www.ffhs .org.uk and click its Find a Society link, shown in Figure 5-2. FFHS has more than 160 member societies. Other societies can be found using the Societies & Groups page of Cyndi's List (http://www.cyndislist.com/societies). You can also do a Google search for the location you're interested in and "genealogy society."

If you join a local society and attend its meetings, find out whether it has a special interest group (SIG) for discussing brick wall problems, such as the one listed by the Florida Genealogical Society (Tampa) as shown in Figure 5-3. Even if it doesn't, the society may provide time during its meetings for its members to ask questions. You can also take advantage of the time before and after the meetings to socialize with other genealogists and share your brick wall problem with them.

If you join a distant society, find out whether it has a newsletter, journal, blog, electronic mailing list, or other means

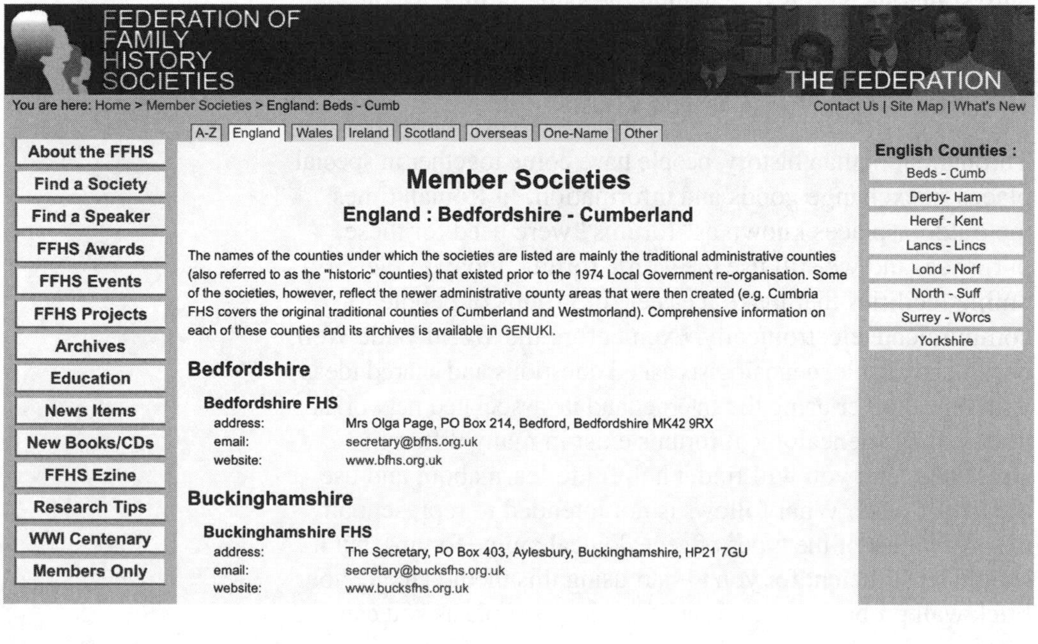

FIGURE 5-2 Federation of Family History Societies—Find a Society

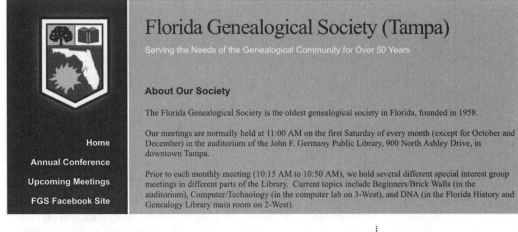

Florida Genealogical Society (Tampa)

Serving the Needs of the Genealogical Community for Over 50 Years

Home

Annual Conference

Upcoming Meetings

FGS Facebook Site

About Our Society

The Florida Genealogical Society is the oldest genealogical society in Florida, founded in 1958.

Our meetings are normally held at 11:00 AM on the first Saturday of every month (except for October and December) in the auditorium of the John F. Germany Public Library, 900 North Ashley Drive, in downtown Tampa.

Prior to each monthly meeting (10:15 AM to 10:50 AM), we hold several different special interest group meetings in different parts of the Library. Current topics include Beginners/Brick Walls (in the auditorium), Computer/Technology (in the computer lab on 3-West), and DNA (in the Florida History and Genealogy Library main room on 2-West).

FIGURE 5-3 Florida Genealogical Society (Tampa) Brick Wall SIG

to get your brick wall problem in front of the membership. Keep in mind that these members are likely to have ancestors in the same geographic area and may have some familiarity with your own family. If other people read about your brick wall problem in the society's newsletter, journal, blog, or mailing list, they may contact you with information or an idea that you can use to solve your problem. You may also make contact with someone who is researching the same family as you.

Online Forums—An Overview

Throughout human history, people have come together in special places to exchange goods and information. In Roman times, the outdoor places known as "forums" were used for these purposes, and we still use the word "forum" today to identify online facilities that make it easier for groups of people to communicate electronically. Even before the World Wide Web became available, genealogists asked questions and shared ideas with one another using the Internet and its associated networks. Today, these genealogical forums exist in many different structures, and you will find it helpful to learn about and use the major ones. What follows is not intended to represent an exhaustive list of the types of genealogical online forums, but it should be sufficient for you to start using this method to get your brick wall problem out in front of as many people as you can.

Electronic Mailing Lists

Although e-mail as we know it today has existed since at least the early 1970s, it was not feasible to send a single e-mail message to a large group of other e-mail users (ones whose e-mail addresses you didn't already know) until the development of electronic mailing list software in the mid-1980s. By 1987, the first genealogy mailing list, ROOTS-L, had been created, and its overwhelming success led to the creation of additional genealogy mailing lists, the vast majority of which are hosted on the RootsWeb website at http://lists.rootsweb.ancestry.com, shown in Figure 5-4. Today, there are more than 32,000 electronic mailing lists dedicated to the discussion of genealogy topics. Most of these are intended to discuss either individual surnames or specific geographic areas, such as U.S. counties. There are, however, mailing lists on many other subjects, including DNA and different types of records research.

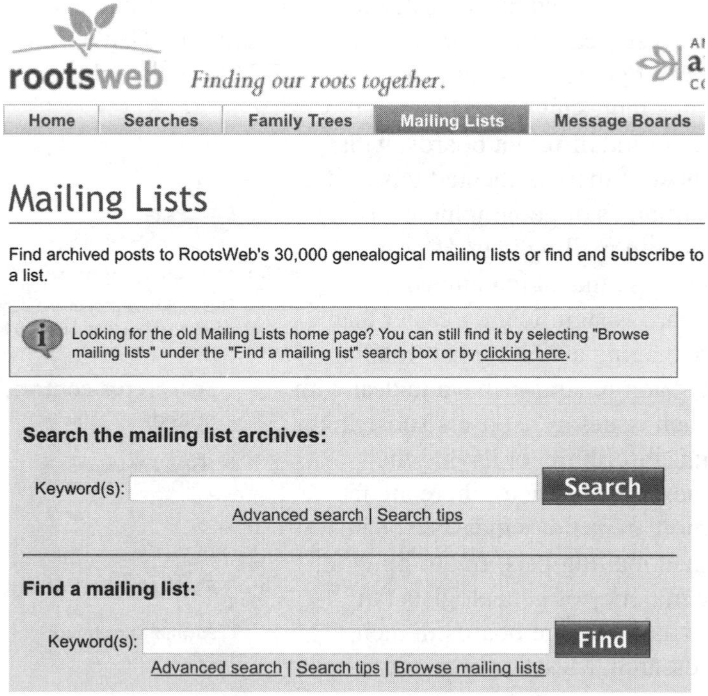

rootsweb *Finding our roots together.*

| Home | Searches | Family Trees | **Mailing Lists** | Message Boards |

Mailing Lists

Find archived posts to RootsWeb's 30,000 genealogical mailing lists or find and subscribe to a list.

Looking for the old Mailing Lists home page? You can still find it by selecting "Browse mailing lists" under the "Find a mailing list" search box or by clicking here.

Search the mailing list archives:

Keyword(s): [   ] Search

Advanced search | Search tips

Find a mailing list:

Keyword(s): [   ] Find

Advanced search | Search tips | Browse mailing lists

FIGURE 5-4 RootsWeb Mailing Lists

Electronic Message Boards

Another major type of online forum is the electronic message board, sometimes referred to as a bulletin board. Just as the electronic mailing list brings to mind the paper-based idea of giving information to an organization that then makes copies and sends them to everyone on its postal mailing list, the electronic message board analogy brings to mind the corkboards found in offices, schools, and homes where people can post a message that they know can be seen by many others. Early forms of international message boards from the 1980s include FidoNet, which linked local dial-up bulletin board systems, and Usenet, which originally linked a number of universities and large companies.

Note   Some use the word "forum" or "Internet forum" to refer only to message boards and not to mailing lists.

Today, the most heavily used message boards hosted on the Web include the two large genealogical message board systems owned by Ancestry.com: the Message Boards at Ancestry.com (http://boards.ancestry.com) and GenForum (http://genforum.com). (See Figure 5-5.) Together, these sites represent several hundred thousand different boards, with most of these dedicated to specific surnames or geographic areas, just as with mailing lists. However, because managing a message board is significantly easier than managing a mailing list (mailing list administrators have to deal with such issues as list users subscribing, unsubscribing, or having their messages bounce), there are far more genealogy message boards than mailing lists. In our opinion, a majority of genealogists fail to use message boards in their research. Message boards can be an

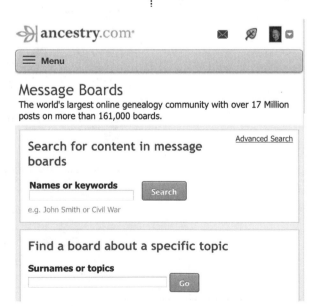

FIGURE 5-5 Ancestry.com Message Boards

invaluable resource, and failing to use them can be a grievous mistake. You never know who is researching your ancestry and whose collaboration could make the difference between a brick wall and research progress.

Facebook Groups, Google+ Communities, and Genealogy Wise

The overwhelming popularity of Facebook (over 1 billion active users at the time of this writing) has not escaped the notice of genealogists, many of whom were already using it to keep in touch with relatives, friends, and long-lost schoolmates. When Facebook released its Group feature in 2010, genealogists began creating Groups based around specific geographic areas and ethnic research. Some genealogy-related Groups have more than 3,000 members, while others have fewer than 100. Within each Group, Facebook members can post messages, add photos and videos, upload files, and search the postings. Some Groups require approval from a group administrator before allowing you to join. In an open Group, anyone (even non-members) can see the postings made by the members, while in a closed Group only members can see the postings. Many Groups that relate to genealogical research are open Groups so that non-members can discover its messages. (It is even possible to have a secret Group, whose existence isn't visible in a search, but this type of Group is less likely to be of value to the typical genealogical researcher.) Figure 5-6 shows the beginning of the list of Facebook genealogy Groups. You can view this entire list by typing the word "genealogy" in the search box at the top of the Facebook page. When the search results page is displayed, click on the Groups link in the left hand column. This will display the list of those groups. You can browse the list, and join or request to join those Groups of interest to you.

The newer Google+ social media site released its Communities feature in December 2012. (See Figure 5-7.) Resembling Facebook Groups, Google+ Communities allows the postings of messages, photos, and videos. Unlike

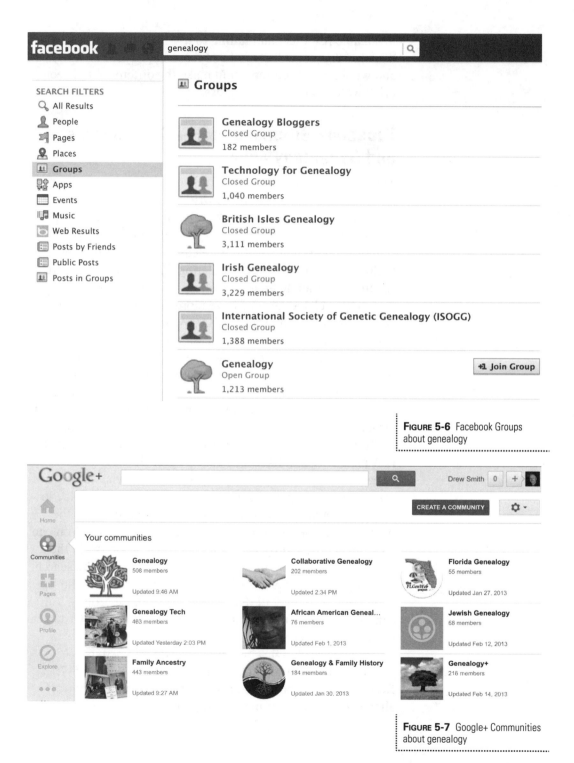

FIGURE 5-6   Facebook Groups about genealogy

FIGURE 5-7   Google+ Communities about genealogy

Facebook Groups, Google+ Communities have no built-in way to share files, but you can always link to a file shared via Google Drive, Dropbox, or a similar file-sharing site. Because Google+ Communities have not been around as long as Facebook Groups, and because Google+ has far fewer active members than Facebook, there are fewer genealogy-related Communities than there are Groups, and genealogy-related Communities tend to have fewer members. (The largest genealogy-related Community on Google+ has approximately 800 members, and most have only a few hundred or less.)

Founded in 2009, the social site GenealogyWise (http://www.genealogywise.com) (Figure 5-8) not only predates the existence of Facebook Groups, but also devotes itself entirely to genealogy. While GenealogyWise can't boast the hundreds of millions of users found on Facebook or Google+, it does provide a place where genealogists can focus on their research without the distractions found on the more popular sites. GenealogyWise has over 4,000 groups (many oriented toward specific surnames), although the largest have only about 1,000 members, and most have only a few hundred or fewer.

FIGURE 5-8 GenealogyWise

Finding the Most Relevant Online Forum

Posting a brick wall problem to an online forum begins with figuring out the best forum in which to post. Between the mailing lists, message boards, and social media groups, there are well over 200,000 different genealogy forums. You want to select the forum or forums that are most relevant to your problem, in the hope of attracting the attention of those who are most likely to have the knowledge and skills to offer you useful information and ideas. For the typical brick wall problem, there are three categories of forums that you should look into: surnames, geographic areas, and ethnicities.

The largest numbers of forums, primarily those found as mailing lists, message boards, and GenealogyWise groups, are based on surname. We estimate that there are a few thousand surname-based groups on GenealogyWise, more than 20,000 surname-based mailing lists, and more than 150,000 surname-based message boards. Given that there are more than several hundred million different surnames in the world, only the most common are likely to have their own group, mailing list, or message board. (If one for your surname of interest doesn't already exist, don't rule out the idea of starting your own.) As you are looking for a forum related to your brick wall problem, keep in mind that some surname-oriented forums handle different spellings of the same surname. Because your brick wall problem may involve more than one surname, look for forums for each surname that ties closely to your problem. In addition, search for your surname on message boards devoted to the geographic location where your ancestor lived.

The second largest number of genealogy forums are geographically oriented. You will find forums at the country level, the state (or equivalent) level, and the county (or equivalent) level. Because political and administrative boundaries change over time, consider not only the geographic area that was in existence at the time period of your brick wall problem, but also the geographic area that exists today. If your brick wall problem involves people living near an administrative border, also consider posting your problem to a forum for the area right across the border. Posting your query in two places may attract the interest of people who know something about the cross-boundary history and people.

Finally, your brick wall problem may involve individuals of a particularly relevant ethnic or religious group. Because there are forums dedicated to such groups, use these to get your problem out in front of experts knowledgeable about the surnames, geographic areas, record types, and cultural practices associated with the relevant group. They may provide you with suggestions for other research paths.

Whenever it is appropriate, consider posting your brick wall problem to multiple forums. Perhaps you have an ancestor who lived in the western part of Orange County, North Carolina, in the last quarter of the eighteenth century. That county was split to create Caswell County in 1777, and Caswell County was split in 1791 to create Person County. You might therefore want to post your brick wall ancestor's information to the surname forum, as well as to the forums for Orange, Caswell, and Person Counties. This will improve your chances of making contact with someone who may have information about your ancestor in the times when the different county governments had responsibility for the area where you ancestor lived.

The Etiquette of Online Forums

When you are interacting with others in a genealogical forum, you are dealing with an unknown number of strangers. In that situation, you want to make a good first impression. Although genealogists are usually patient with beginners, they are more willing to go the extra mile for those who enter the forum in a polite manner and who demonstrate that they have done their homework. In this section, we'll review some tips on forum etiquette that will smooth the communication process and increase the likelihood that you'll get the help you need.

Before you even post in the forum, you have to consider whether or not you're in the right forum. In the previous section, we discussed how to find the most relevant forums in which to post. It is irritating to forum readers to see someone post a query or problem that has nothing to do with the surname or geographic area that the forum is supposed to be about. Also, if you are posting your problem to a forum for a particular geographic area, make certain that you are posting at the right level. What we mean is that if you are fairly certain that you know what county your problem involves, post the problem in the forum for that county, and not at the forum for the entire state. If you don't know what county is relevant to your question, then post your query to the forum intended for state-level discussions, and don't spam your posting to every county forum for that state.

Once you know that are you in the right forum, search the forum to see if your question has been asked before. You may find that your individual or family of interest has already been discussed, or that someone else has asked about the whereabouts of certain kinds of records for the geographic area of interest. If your question has not been well addressed, go ahead and post your question, but you may want to comment in your posting that you have searched the forum's archive and haven't located any information relevant to your question.

Messages posted to lists and boards use subject lines, just like personal e-mail, and you should spend some time in crafting the best possible subject line to briefly and adequately describe your brick wall problem. Subject lines that provide no useful content, such as "Help!" or "Looking for great-grandmother," will annoy many forum users, who lack the time or interest to open and read every message. Forum users depend upon the subject line to determine whether or not they will be able to help with the problem. If you are posting your brick wall problem to a surname-oriented forum, then help the potential reader by identifying a geographic area, first name, and/or time period in the subject line. In the case of a forum for a geographic area, your subject line should identify the surname of interest and, where possible, a more specific location, such as the name of a town within the county. You may also include a range of years to help the reader understand your focus. The subject line does not need to be a complete sentence, and you should make liberal use of understandable abbreviations to keep it as short as possible. In a subject line, it may help to write surnames in all caps, especially in cases where the surname could be confused with a given name. Here are some examples of good subject lines, some of which use common abbreviations.

- **Reuben MORGAN - NC – ca. 1740s**   This subject indicates that the contents concern one Reuben Morgan who lived in North Carolina in the 1740s.

- **John SWORDS - SC>GA>AL>GA**   This subject indicates that the contents concern a John Swords who migrated from South Carolina to Georgia to Alabama and back to Georgia. The implication is that the writer has traced the movements and is seeking more information.

- **African-American Marriages, Greene County, Georgia: 1878–1883**   The writer is seeking information about marriage records in a specific area during a particular time period.

- **James MORGAN b. 1645 in Nantmel, Radnor, Wales, married to Jane EVANS b. 1647**   This writer included the names of both persons, the birth years of both individuals, and the origin of the male.

The body of your message is as important as the subject line. Lay out your brick wall problem in as organized a manner as you can, and be extremely clear as to what your research question is. If you are looking for the maiden name of a married woman, or the names of the parents of an ancestor, say so specifically. If you need the location or date for a birth, marriage, death, or burial, then make that clear. Try not to ramble so that the reader won't have to guess what your brick wall problem is.

Be sure to include the information that you already know is relevant to the problem, and explain how you know it, in case a respondent wants to question the credibility of the information. If you have already searched specific books, online databases, or physical record collections, you should identify them. Forum readers don't want to waste time offering ideas for research that has already been pursued by the person posting the query. Don't make readers feel like they are pulling teeth just to get you to provide details about your problem so that they can give you helpful ideas.

Because message boards and social networking groups link your query to your online profile, you do not usually need to sign your postings, although there is no harm in signing it with your name. In the case of mailing lists, avoid putting anything at the end of your messages other than your name and e-mail address. Genealogy forum readers don't need to see your favorite decorative graphic or an inspirational, political, or religious quote. Save those for your forum profile or personal e-mail. In particular, do not use a signature that includes a list of every surname you are researching. Such lists may cause false hits when someone is searching the mailing list archives or message board for a surname or combination of surnames.

Finally, be sure that people will be able to contact you in the future. Avoid changing the e-mail address you use for genealogical research. If you must change it, return to the forums where you originally posted your problems and reply to them, indicating your new e-mail address. In this way, no one who has a potential solution to your brick wall problem will become frustrated because they can't reach you. Likewise, if you encounter a post and try to contact someone whose e-mail address is no longer valid, search the forum for the author's name or a username. The person may have posted a change of contact address there.

Blogs, Wikis, and Podcasts

There are far more ways to share genealogical information online beyond simply using a mailing list, message board, or social networking group, and some of these ways can contribute toward finding your brick wall solution.

Blogs

Depending upon who is doing the writing and what is being written about, a blog can resemble either a newspaper/newsletter or a diary/journal. In the hands of a genealogist, a blog can be used as a research log, documenting for the world what has been found and what remains to be discovered.

Because blog content is normally indexed by the major search engines, blog postings can be stumbled upon by anyone doing a typical Web search, which means that brick wall questions about specific ancestors or places can be found by others researching the same names or locations. Also, blogs can be set up so that interested readers can comment on blog entries, and these comments may take the form of questions, answers, or ideas related to the brick wall problem being presented. A genealogy blog can, such as Drew's blog shown in Figure 5-9, include ancestral photos and digital images of documents. We have frequently seen bloggers posting images of hard-to-read documents, sometimes written in languages other than English, and using the power of crowdsourcing to determine what the document says.

Wikis

If a blog is like a newspaper, then a wiki is like an encyclopedia. While it is highly unlikely that any long-time user of the Web has failed to hear of Wikipedia, what is certainly possible is that

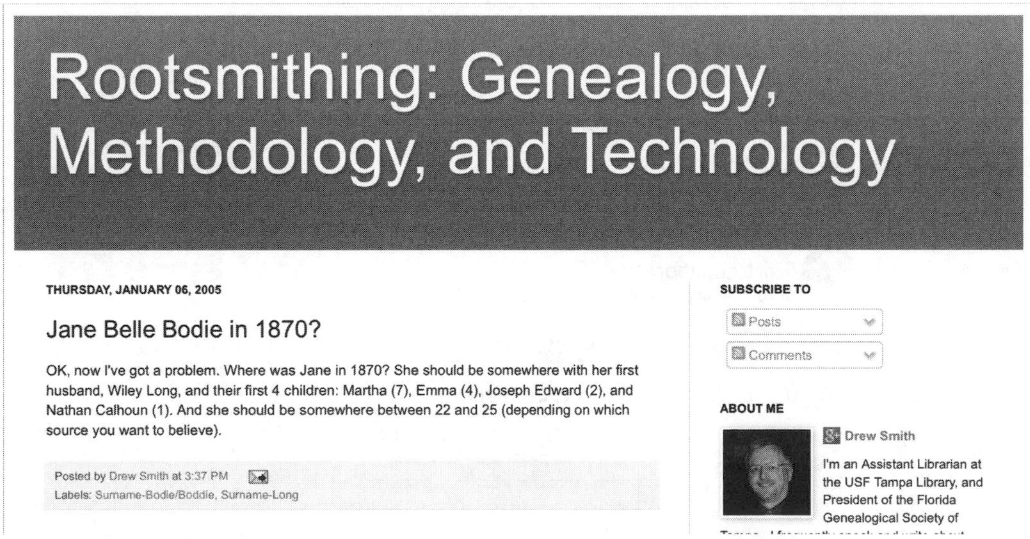

Rootsmithing: Genealogy, Methodology, and Technology

THURSDAY, JANUARY 06, 2005

Jane Belle Bodie in 1870?

OK, now I've got a problem. Where was Jane in 1870? She should be somewhere with her first husband, Wiley Long, and their first 4 children: Martha (7), Emma (4), Joseph Edward (2), and Nathan Calhoun (1). And she should be somewhere between 22 and 25 (depending on which source you want to believe).

Posted by Drew Smith at 3:37 PM
Labels: Surname-Bodie/Boddie, Surname-Long

SUBSCRIBE TO

Posts
Comments

ABOUT ME

 Drew Smith

I'm an Assistant Librarian at the USF Tampa Library, and President of the Florida Genealogical Society of

FIGURE 5-9 Rootsmithing—
a personal research blog

some genealogists are unaware that there are wikis designed specifically for genealogical information. Some, such as WeRelate (http://www.werelate.org shown in Figure 5-10), serve primarily as information about specific individuals, while others, such as the FamilySearch Research Wiki (https://www.familysearch.org/learn/wiki/en/Main_Page shown in Figure 5-11) and the Ancestry.com Family History Wiki (http://www.ancestry.com/wiki/index.php?title=Main_Page shown in Figure 5-12), provide genealogy-related reference material for geographic areas, record types, and methodologies. Anyone dealing with a brick wall problem might benefit from reviewing the content provided by genealogy wikis. Cyndi's List includes links to a number of other genealogy-related wikis.

FIGURE 5-10 WeRelate

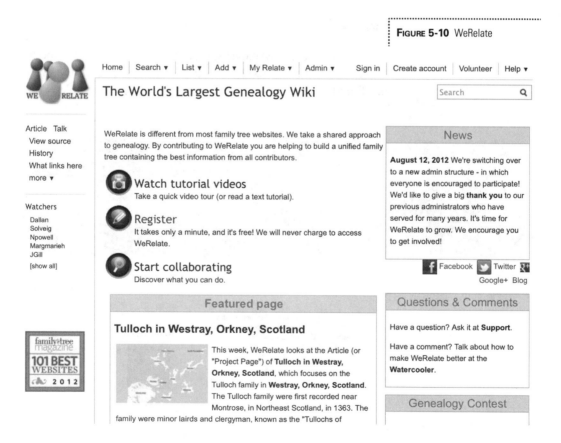

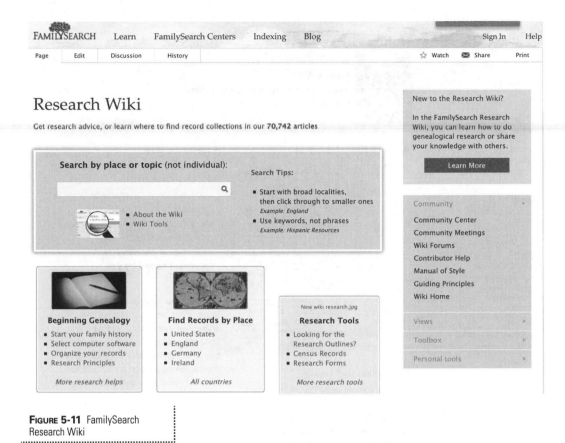

Figure 5-11 FamilySearch
Research Wiki

Podcasts

Podcasts present pre-recorded audio (and sometimes video) programs and are made available on the Web. They became a regular part of the world of genealogy in 2005 with the introduction of our own *Genealogy Guys Podcast* (online at http://genealogyguys.com and shown in Figure 5-13). As a result, many thousands of genealogists around the world have enjoyed a growing archive of audio material that they can listen to whenever and wherever convenient. Because we read and respond to listener e-mail, and because one listener's brick wall problem is heard by thousands of other genealogists, it is not unusual for listeners to send their solutions and ideas to The Genealogy Guys to share with the person who contributed the original problem.

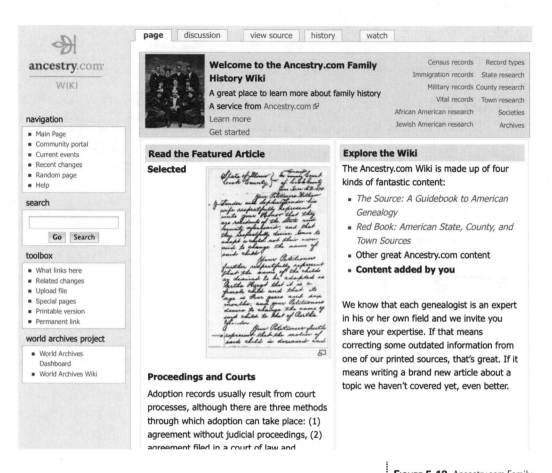

FIGURE 5-12 Ancestry.com Family History Wiki

Example 1

One of the listeners of *The Genealogy Guys Podcast* reported that she was struggling to read her grandfather's handwriting on a family document that she had acquired. She decided to post a scanned image of the document on Facebook. She reported that, within an hour, the document had been translated and transcribed through the efforts of friends from New Jersey to California. None of these people were genealogists; they were just friends who were up for a challenge.

The Genealogy Guys Podcast

George G. Morgan and Drew Smith discuss genealogy. This is the longest-running, regularly produced genealogy podcast in the world!

Wed, 13 February 2013

The Genealogy Guys Podcast #247 – 2013 February 10

Drew, an official RootsTech 2013 blogger, reminds listeners that Early Bird Registration for RootsTech 2013 ends on February 15th. Drew invites our listeners to email us at genealogyguys@gmail.com with suggestions for interviews while he's at RootsTech 2013.

Other news includes:

- RootsMagic announces a free viewer app for the iPhone, iPad, and iPod Touch.
- BillionGraves has been acquired by Otter Creek Holdings.
- Findmypast.com adds 21 million new Irish birth, marriage, and death records.
- The "Find My Past" TV show from the UK, seasons 1 and 2, is available for viewing online at http://www.findmypast.com/articles/find-my-past-tv/series-two.
- Ancestry.com has updated the 1850 and 1940 U.S. federal censuses online.
- The Federation of Genealogical Societies has launched a new blog for the War of 1812 fundraising at http://www.preservethepensions.org/blog/.
- MyHeritage has launched a special campaign offering deep discounts on DNA tests through Family Tree DNA. They also have released a

The Genealogy Guys
Drew (l) and George (r)

Drew and RootsTech 2013

Search

	Search

Figure 5-13 The Genealogy Guys Podcast

Example 2

As mentioned earlier, many genealogical societies host or facilitate one or more SIGs that focus on particular topics of interest to their members. The Lee County Genealogical Society (http://www.leecountygenealogy.org) in Fort Myers, Florida, hosts 13 SIGs, including those centered on English, Irish, German, Midwest, New York/New England, and Quebec research, and groups concerning the use of Family Tree Maker and RootsMagic software programs.

The Florida Genealogical Society (of Tampa) (http://fgstampa.org) currently hosts three SIGs prior to their regular monthly meetings: Beginners and Brick Walls, Computers and Technology, and DNA. At one of its Beginners and Brick Walls gathering, questions were raised about U.S. naturalization records. One attendee had obtained a digitized index card for an ancestor's naturalization file. During the course of that SIG meeting, the group learned how to locate and order copies of the naturalization files at appropriate NARA facilities. They also learned about online sites at which digitized and indexed documents are being made available. The facilitator also cited books and online sources where more information can be found.

Example 3

Drew had a brick wall problem involving the maiden name of his paternal grandmother's mother, Sarah, wife of Louis Weinglass. Some records, such as the SS-5 for Louis and Sarah's son Jack, said that his mother's maiden name was Grodowitz. But other records, such as an online index for marriages in New York City, said that Louis Weinglass had married Sarah Levy. Were Sarah Grodowitz and Sarah Levy the same person, or two different people?

Drew chose to post his question to the Jewish Genealogy community on Google+. Another poster pointed out that Drew was using the marriage index as his source, but that Drew had not obtained a copy of the original marriage document. The poster also pointed out that Sarah could have been married to a Levy before she married Louis Weinglass.

Example 4

One of George's longest standing brick walls involved trying to locate information about his great-uncle, Brisco Washington Holder. Brisco left his native Rome, Georgia, around 1906. Family legend said that he died "in the mid-1920s someplace in the Midwest beginning with a C." A listener to The Genealogy Guys Podcast found the death certificate for Brisco online in the Missouri Digital Heritage website. Brisco had died in St. Louis, not in the 1920s but on 17 May 1949. George had never thought to check Missouri records, but this document opened the door to a great number of additional research opportunities. He was able to locate Brisco's burial site and arrange for the placement of a gravestone.

Summary

Genealogy is a social hobby. We might be tempted to think of a genealogical researcher working alone, either at home in front of a computer screen, and with a pile of papers and books, or in a library, archive, or other repository, stopping only to ask a question or make a request of the librarian or archivist. But the reality is that good genealogical research benefits by the sharing of research problems with the broadest possible audience. Those who enjoy face-to-face communication should join their local genealogy society and share their brick wall problem as part of the usual society activities, while those who enjoy online communication can seek out groups of genealogists on mailing lists, message boards, and social networking sites. No genealogist can afford to omit any of the electronic tools in the research process.

The best practice is to be well prepared to explain the brick wall problem, leaving out nothing important, and to listen carefully and thoughtfully to the information and ideas offered by those who take their own time to study the problem and respond. By observing appropriate etiquette and by choosing the appropriate venues, the researcher can benefit greatly from the results of crowdsourcing their problem.

6
Apply Technological Solutions

If you were to find yourself in that deep forest confronted by a high brick wall, you might immediately think to yourself, "If only I had a ladder!" Human beings are very good at inventing, designing, and implementing technological solutions to their problems.

For thousands of years, genealogists have taken advantage of existing technologies and applied them to their research. Before the invention of writing, family historians had to depend upon oral history for the transmission of family information from generation to generation. Once there was the ability to preserve this kind of information in a relatively permanent form, family histories could be written down and illustrated with charts. The printing press made it possible to quickly and easily produce numerous copies of family histories that could be dispersed to various personal collections and libraries. Family history books and other kinds of genealogical documents were made more useful with the invention and application of indexing techniques.

As photography came into common use in the nineteenth century, family historians used it to take family photos. The next big technological leap forward for genealogical research was the beginning of the use of microfilm in the late 1920s and early 1930s to preserve newspapers and other materials, and by 1938, the Genealogical Society of Utah (GSU), the founding organization behind FamilySearch, was microfilming materials for genealogical purposes.

Many of us alive today have lived through the earliest applications of computer technology to genealogical research. Once there were a sufficient number of personal computers in the late 1970s and early 1980s, genealogy software programs began to appear, and it is the rare genealogist today who does not already have such a program on their own desktop or laptop computer. In Chapter 1, we discussed the importance of using a genealogy database program for recording all of the information you have, in order to avoid overlooking any details that may be keys to solving your brick wall problem.

In this chapter, we turn our attention to two technologies that you may not yet have applied to your own research: DNA testing and specialized genealogical software.

DNA Testing: A Very Brief History

Although the chemical molecule we now call "DNA" was first known to biological researchers in the nineteenth century, it would be the early 1950s before scientists were able to confirm that DNA was the molecule responsible for transmitting inheritable biological traits from one generation to the next, such as eye color or blood type. Despite the fact that biologists began to understand that every DNA molecule consisted of a unique sequence of small molecular components known as nucleotides, and that DNA nucleotides came in only four possible variations in terms of their base components (adenine, guanine, cytosine, and thymine, commonly abbreviated as A, G, C, and T), it was not until the early 1970s that it became possible for biological researchers to perform DNA sequencing. Sequencing allowed scientists to determine the exact order of the nucleotides in a DNA sample. (See Figure 6-1.)

Note   Although DNA is found in every kind of known living organism on Earth, from the simplest bacteria to the far more complex fungi, plants, and animals, the rest of this chapter will focus almost exclusively on human DNA.

Obviously, the DNA in your body must resemble, to some degree, the DNA of any other human being, as it is the DNA that gives us the observable biological traits we use to identify a living organism as human. In fact, the DNA sequences of any two humans alive today are nearly identical (and even perfectly identical in the case of identical twins). But when we set aside the 99.9 percent of the DNA in our bodies that is identical to that of all other humans, the part that identifies us as human, we are still left with a tiny percentage that is unique to each of us.

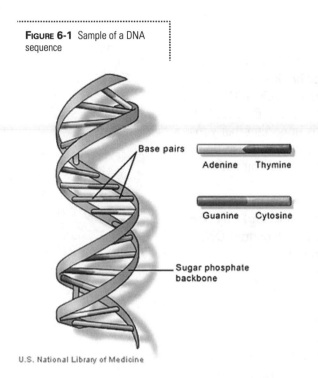

Figure 6-1 Sample of a DNA sequence

Base pairs

Adenine   Thymine

Guanine   Cytosine

Sugar phosphate
backbone

U.S. National Library of Medicine

By the late 1980s, the technology had advanced to the point where it was possible to identify and measure these areas of DNA variation (known as markers), and within a decade it was put to use to provide a unique DNA profile, a genetic fingerprint that could be used to identify not only criminals but also the otherwise unidentified victims of crimes, accidents, and acts of war. Today, several different national government DNA databases exist that contain millions of DNA profiles, and we have become familiar with their use on popular forensic TV shows. Within the United States, the Combined DNA Index System, popularly known as CODIS, is funded by the FBI and used primarily by law enforcement agencies, and has approximately 12 million unique DNA profiles. In the United Kingdom, the UK National Criminal Intelligence DNA Database, commonly known as NDNAD, will contain more than 6 million unique DNA profiles by the time you read this. It is important to realize that these national government DNA databases are useful for matching known individuals to DNA samples found at a particular location (such as a crime scene), but they provide no significant genealogical benefit and are not available to genealogical researchers.

So how is this applicable to genealogical research? Although any particular genetic marker, by definition, varies in its genetic makeup from one human to the next, we inherit our own copy of markers from our parents. And because our parents inherited their markers from their own parents, and so on back in time through the generations, these markers provide a technological way to link us to our near and distant relatives.

Types of DNA Testing

Before you can determine whether or not DNA testing can be helpful in solving your genealogical brick wall, you first have to understand that there are different kinds of DNA tests and that each kind of test has applications to different kinds of genealogical research problems. It is important that you fully understand what each test can and cannot do, so that you won't spend money on a test that will provide you with no significant possible benefit.

Every human cell (except for red blood cells) contains DNA, and that DNA falls into two types: nuclear DNA (the DNA found in the cell's nucleus), and mitochondrial DNA (the DNA found in the cell's mitochondria).

mtDNA Testing

The mitochondria are a type of organelle (a subunit of a biological cell that performs a particular function). Each human cell may have as few as one or as many as several thousand mitochondria, and these mitochondria provide a source of chemical energy to the entire cell. The mtDNA is completely separate from the cell's nuclear DNA, as shown in Figure 6-2. Although mtDNA is present in both the sperm and egg cells prior to human conception, only the mtDNA from the egg cell is preserved after conception, which means that our mtDNA is a copy of our mother's mtDNA. And our mother's mtDNA is a copy of her own mother's mtDNA, and so on back through the generations from daughter to mother.

Could mtDNA testing solve a genealogical brick wall problem? Yes, in certain specialized cases. In the first case, let us imagine that you and another researcher have each traced your ancestry back a number of generations to a Mary Smith living in a small town, and you are wondering whether it is the same Mary Smith or two different women with the same name. If you, or another of your living relatives, are descended from your Mary Smith through a strictly female line (child-to-mother-to-mother, and so on), and the other genealogical researcher (or another of their own living relatives) is descended from their Mary Smith in the same way, you could arrange for an mtDNA test for a descendant from each branch. If the

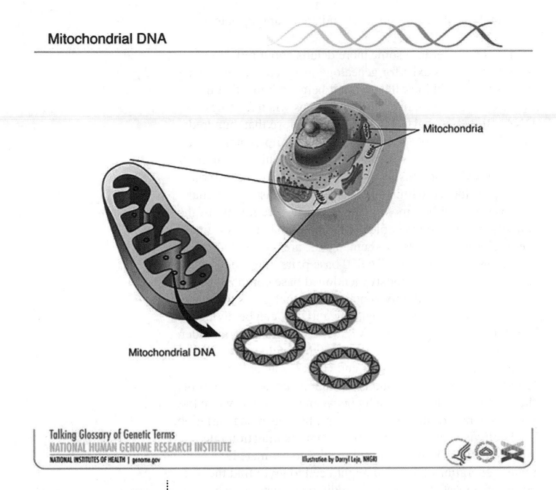

Mitochondrial DNA

Mitochondria

Mitochondrial DNA

Talking Glossary of Genetic Terms
NATIONAL HUMAN GENOME RESEARCH INSTITUTE
NATIONAL INSTITUTES OF HEALTH | genome.gov

Illustration by Darryl Leja, NHGRI

FIGURE 6-2 Mitochondrial DNA

mtDNA test results match, you have good reason to believe that you are descended from the same Mary Smith, and if they don't match, you have good reason to believe that there were two different women with that name. (Just to be careful here, even if the mtDNA does match, it would not prove with 100 percent certainty that the two Mary Smiths were the same woman. For instance, if there were two Mary Smiths who were first cousins through their mothers, a matching test would not rule out that possibility.)

A similar scenario would involve wondering if your maternal-line ancestor was a sister to someone else's maternal-line ancestor (perhaps both ancestors from the same location have the same surname and are of appropriate ages to be sisters).

Let's now get into some more details about mtDNA, what test options exist for genealogy researchers, and what the results would look like. First, it helps to know that the mitochondria are relatively simple things when it comes to DNA. Biologists have good reason to believe that, hundreds of millions of years ago, the ancestors of mitochondria were bacteria that developed a symbiotic relationship with more complex living organisms (animals), and the mitochondria took up residence within animals cells. Because the animal cells were providing most of the necessary life functions, the mitochondria could become even simpler than they originally were. The mitochondria in human cells are so simple that the mtDNA is only about 16,000 base pairs long (the base pairs being those previously mentioned base components A, G, C, and T), and only contains 37 actual genes that have a biological function. Biologically, mtDNA can be divided into three distinct regions: HVR1, HVR2, and the remainder, known as the coding region (the part that includes the 37 genes). The "HVR" in HVR1 and HVR2 is an abbreviation for "hypervariable region," and is so named because this part of the mtDNA tends to vary a lot between individuals while the non-HVR part of the mtDNA doesn't have as much variation.

Biologists have studied mtDNA and its mutation rate, which enables DNA testing companies to estimate how many generations back you might need to go to find the common ancestor between two individuals who have a matching mtDNA test. For instance, if two individuals have a matching HVR1 test, it is estimated that there is a 50 percent chance that their common maternal ancestor lived within the most recent 52 generations. As you can imagine, this isn't especially useful for figuring out a genealogical relationship between two test subjects.

What if we add on the HVR2 test to the mix, and the two individuals still match perfectly? This helps a bit, bringing us a 50 percent chance of being in the most recent 28 generations. However, given that this is still something like 700 years ago, it is fairly unlikely that the two modern descendants are going to have a paper trail that far back that will enable them to figure out the exact relationship.

Finally, what if you test the full mtDNA genome, including the coding region? Before we talk about the results, it should be pointed out that, because the full mtDNA genome test includes testing the 37 genes that code for biological proteins, the results could potentially point to health-related issues. If you have any possible concerns about knowing these kinds of results that could identify genetic diseases or susceptibility to disease, you will want to give serious consideration before having this test done. (The issue here is not about whether the testing company will disclose this information to anyone else, including insurance companies or employers, but about whether you are comfortable with having his information about yourself.)

As it turns out, a full mtDNA genome match between two individuals would identify a 50 percent likelihood that the two individuals have a common maternal-line ancestor in the most recent five generations. Finally, we are within the realm where many genealogical researchers have a paper trail.

Drew had a full mtDNA genome test completed in early September of 2012. As of the time of this writing, he has over 1,900 matches at the HVR1 level, and nearly 300 matches at the combined HVR1 and HVR2 level. But when you look at his matches for the full mtDNA genome, Drew has only 1 perfect match. The individual who matches Drew has his family tree uploaded to the testing services website (as does Drew), but so far, there are no matching names in the maternal line, although they do share the geographic location of South Carolina. Unfortunately, the matching individual has not yet responded to requests from Drew for contact. (Just because someone matches you does not mean that they are still active in their genealogical research or that they will respond to genealogical queries.) Nevertheless, this match may someday provide an additional clue for Drew to break through his brick wall in this maternal line.

Setting aside the issue of matching another individual, how do you go about interpreting your personal mtDNA test results? Clearly, it would be cumbersome if you had to get your test report in the form of a list of over 16,000 letters (the A, G, T, and C). In the 1970s, a group of scientists at Cambridge University did a full mtDNA genome test of an individual (someone with European ancestry), and

the results of this test became known as the Cambridge
Reference Sequence (CRS). Later, some errors in the testing
and reporting process were discovered, so a new version of
the CRS was published in 1999 and became known as the
rCRS (revised CRS). This meant that any future tests of other
individuals could be reported by simply noting the differences
between the new individual and the original CRS test subject.
Because mtDNA changes fairly slowly, individuals who are
descended from Europeans are likely to have only a small
number of differences from the CRS, but individuals with
ancestry from other parts of the world might have a large
number of differences.

Later in this chapter there's a more detailed discussion of
"Mitochondrial Eve" but, at this point, let's just realize that
it would be much more fair to figure out what the mtDNA
should have looked like for the woman who is the maternal-
line direct ancestor of all humans alive today, and to report
our mtDNA results by saying how they would differ from
that distant ancestor. This means that the report for Europeans
(and their descendants) would be a bit longer, but the report
for individuals from other parts of the world would be a
lot shorter. This new standard, the Reconstructed Sapiens
Reference Sequence (RSRS), was proposed in 2012 and is
now being used as a way to provide the results of mtDNA
testing.

For instance, using the older rCRS method, Drew has 5
differences in his HVR1, 4 differences in his HVR2, and 27
differences in his coding region. Using the new RSRS method,
Drew has 11 differences in his HVR1, 8 differences in his
HVR2, and 45 differences in his coding region. On average,
all living human beings will have about the same total number
of differences in their full mtDNA genome using the RSRS
method but, of course, the more closely any two individuals
are related via their maternal-only line, the more closely their
list of RSRS values will match.

Y-DNA Testing

Within the nucleus of each human cell is the nuclear
DNA, normally divided into 46 different DNA pieces
known as chromosomes. (Some genetic disorders, such

as Down Syndrome, are caused by an abnormal number of chromosomes. In the case of Down Syndrome, there is an extra copy of one of the chromosomes, specifically chromosome 21.) These 46 chromosomes can be understood to represent 23 pairs, where one chromosome in each pair was inherited from the father, the other from the mother, which means that we get approximately 50 percent of our DNA from one of our parents and the remainder from the other parent. One of these 23 pairs is known as the sex chromosomes, because its makeup determines whether the individual is male or female. The remaining 22 pairs are known as the autosomes. (See Figure 6-3.)

The sex chromosomes come in two varieties: X and Y. In normal humans, an individual has either two X chromosomes (resulting in a female) or one X and one Y (resulting in a male). Therefore, a female child gets one of her X chromosomes from her mother and one from her father, while a male child gets his X chromosome from his mother and his Y chromosome from his father (since only males carry a Y chromosome).

In modern Western cultures, children usually inherit their surname from their father, so a particular Y chromosome and

FIGURE 6-3 Chromosomes

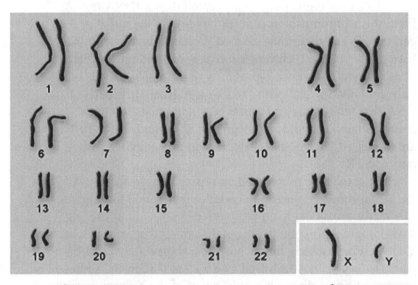

autosomes   sex chromosomes

U.S. National Library of Medicine

a particular surname are usually associated with each other as they are passed from a male to his male children, generation after generation. Exceptions, of course, will occur when adoptions (whether formal or informal) or name changes are involved, or whenever a child is not the biological offspring of his legal father. This type of exception is known as a non-paternity event, or NPE.

Because genealogists so often focus on researching an ancestral line for a given surname in the family, Y-chromosome testing can often provide evidence to support relatedness or lack of relatedness between two living male individuals sharing the same surname. For instance, a brick wall question might involve trying to determine whether two or more Jones families living in the same town at the same time are related to each other or not. By locating living male Jones descendants for each of the known families, and testing their Y-chromosomes, a match can provide support that the families are related, and a failure to match can cast doubt on their relatedness. However, because of the exceptions already mentioned, Y-chromosome testing cannot rule out that descendants are legally related to each other by a common Jones ancestor, but it can establish that the descendants are not biologically related that way.

Y-DNA testing is more complicated than mtDNA testing. First, the Y chromosome is much larger than the mtDNA genome. (Remember that the mtDNA has only about 16,000 base pairs, but the Y chromosome has about 58 million base pairs). Therefore, genealogical tests of the Y-DNA focus on only a relatively small set of markers. Markers (the parts of DNA that tend to vary a lot between individuals) on the Y chromosome fall into two categories: STRs and SNPs. SNPs are discussed later in this chapter, so at this point we'll look only at STRs.

STR stands for "short tandem repeat." There are parts of the Y chromosome that don't code for genes, and those parts can vary a great deal from person to person without causing any biological problem for the male human who carries that Y-DNA. For instance, there could be a short sequence of base pairs (let's say, an A followed by a T) that is repeated some number of times. In other words, a part of the Y chromosome could look like "ATATATAT." Because these sequences are short, tandem (they run together), and repeating, they are known as short tandem repeats, or STRs. In reality, the repeating unit can be anywhere from two base pairs long to up to six base pairs long, and they can repeat anywhere from several times to several dozen times.

Because a son inherits his copy of Y-DNA from his father, the son's Y-DNA should contain the same number of repeats for each marker as his father's Y-DNA had, but because there is always the possibility of a mutation (mutations are discussed in more detail later in the chapter), the son may have a marker in his Y-DNA that has a lower number or a higher number of repeats than his father's corresponding marker had. As the generations go by, the number of repeats for a particular marker may continue to change, with the number continuing to go down or to go up (although it is possible for it to return to a value held by an ancestor before the mutation). Some markers have a relatively slow mutation rate, while other markers have a relatively higher mutation rate, so it is possible to compare the markers of two individuals to see how closely they match.

The earliest Y-DNA tests offered to the general public tested only a limited number of different markers (12 was a common number) but two men matching perfectly on a 12-marker test does not provide much in the way of genealogical information. For instance, Drew had his Y-DNA tested, and his 12 markers match perfectly with over 700 other men in the Family Tree DNA database. According to what is currently known about the mutation rate of the Y chromosome, it is estimated that two men having a perfect 12-marker match have a 50 percent chance of having a common ancestor in the last seven generations. (Drew has a paper trail for his Smith line going back only four generations.)

Clearly, it must be desirable to test more than 12 markers if one is going to find matches with a greater certainty in the time frame of a common paper trail. Drew also had a 37-marker test done. Unfortunately, he had no perfect matches at the 37-marker level, and in fact had only one match at all, a 3-step match (in this case, meaning that Drew's test results had 3 markers that differed by only 1 value from the test results of the other individual). This still puts the common ancestor generations earlier than Drew's paper trail but, on the plus side, the other test subject's ancestor was also a Smith from Ireland, so there remains the possibility of finding out someday how Drew and the other test subject are related.

Today, it is possible to test as many as 67 or even 111 markers, providing a way to achieve extremely good estimates as to how many generations back the common ancestor lived. If a number of living male descendants, already believed to be related, take a 111-marker test, it can help to organize those descendants into the most plausible family tree structure that would account for the mutations seen in the results.

Autosomal DNA Testing

As mentioned in the previous section, the autosomes are the 22 pairs of nuclear chromosomes that exclude the sex-determining chromosomes (X and Y). Although we get approximately 50 percent of our autosomal DNA from each of our parents, it gets more complicated as we go back through the generations. Each individual autosomal chromosome that we inherit from a particular parent is actually a unique combination of the two similar autosomal chromosomes that our parent inherited from their own parents. This is why your own DNA differs from that of your siblings (except for identical twins); you each get different combinations of DNA passed to you from your common parents. Again, on average, you get 25 percent of your DNA from each of your grandparents, and 12.5 percent from each of your great-grandparents, and so forth, but because these are averages and not exact amounts, you may find that you have gotten little or no DNA from one or more of your more distant ancestors.

These percentages also give us an idea of how much DNA we share with our siblings, our first cousins, our second cousins, and so forth. On average, we share 50 percent of our DNA with our siblings, 12.5 percent with our first cousins, 3.125 percent with second cousins, and so on, but again these are averages, not exact amounts, which can vary from one relationship to the next. As you can imagine, this means that using an autosomal DNA test can help adoptees to verify relatedness to a possible biological sibling or half-sibling, or it can help genealogists to verify some level of relationship with first, second, third, or possibly fourth cousins, but as we move into relationships with more distant cousins, autosomal DNA testing may not reveal a relationship, even when it exists, because the two cousins don't share enough DNA in common for the matching DNA to be detected.

Autosomal testing is arguably the most complex kind of DNA testing, primarily because matches between two individuals will not automatically identify how those two individuals are related. On the other hand, it is the only kind of testing that will locate cousins across any possible line (not just the strictly paternal or strictly maternal lines), and it is the only option available to females who have no male relatives alive to take a Y-DNA test but where the female still wants to locate possible cousins along her paternal line.

Drew took an autosomal test with Family Tree DNA (they call their autosomal test "Family Finder"), and he was given an online report indicating the names of nearly 750 individuals with whom he shared some stretch of DNA. Each potentially matching individual had the option of making certain information public, such as a family tree or a list of ancestral surnames. Drew has not yet had the opportunity to make contact with these matches, but each of them represents an opportunity to break through a brick wall in one of Drew's ancestral lines.

With a little extra time and effort, very interesting information can be derived from an autosomal test, especially if it is compared with a test taken by a known close relative, such as a first cousin. For instance, if two first cousins take an autosomal test, and examine the detailed results of their tests, they may be able to figure out exactly which stretches of DNA they inherited from their common grandparents (which means that each tested individual can figure out if the DNA came from their mother or from their father). As more first cousins are tested and the results are compared, a much more accurate chromosome map can be created for the common ancestors, making it easier to figure out how one is related to new individuals who have matching DNA segments.

Deep Ancestry

While tests for mtDNA, Y-DNA, and autosomal DNA can provide estimates of degree of recent relatedness between two or more individuals, something that genealogists are especially interested in, another aspect of DNA testing relates to something that may fall much farther back in time. Some genealogists are very interested in the combination of ethnicities that they have in their personal biological mix, and they may be especially interested in confirming or refuting a family story that some particular ancestor was a member of some particular ethnic population.

As previously mentioned, our autosomal DNA is a mixture from our parents, and through them from each generation before, but the more generations back you go, the chances increase that some particular ancestor will not have contributed any of their DNA to you or to whatever living person you are having tested. This means that even if your distant ancestor of interest was a member of a particular ethnic group, your own DNA test may provide no evidence of it. Or, it is possible that your DNA test will show evidence of a particular ethnic population, but that you are descended from that population via a person in your ancestry different than the one you originally thought.

On the bright side, DNA testing for two of our ancestral lines can take us as far back in time as we like, namely, the strictly maternal line (which mtDNA testing can tell us about) and the strictly paternal line (which Y-DNA testing can tell us about). At this point, we need to learn about mutations, Mitochondrial Eve, Y-chromosomal Adam, haplogroups, SNPs, and a few other somewhat technical biological concepts relating to our deep human ancestry.

Mutations

As we mentioned earlier in this chapter, all humans alive today have almost the exact same DNA as every other human, and only a very small percentage of our DNA differs from person to person. Of course, it is that small amount of variation that makes each of us a unique biological organism. But if there was once only a relatively small population of humans (say, a few hundred thousand years ago), where did all of the genetic variation come from that we see in the billions of humans alive today? While some of it is a mixture of the variation that was already present in the original human population, most of it is the result of chemical changes that can take place during the biological process of reproduction. Given the very large size of the human genome, you should not be surprised that the biological process that copies parental DNA to produce the DNA of the offspring will be an imperfect process, resulting in some number of differences between parental DNA and offspring DNA. These biological changes in the DNA are known as *mutations*.

Mitochondrial Eve

If you were to take every human being alive today, and you were somehow able to trace each of his or her direct maternal lines backward in time until you converged upon a single woman, you would have reached the woman popularly known as Mitochondrial Eve. Although Mitochondrial Eve was not the only human woman alive at the time in which she lived, the other women who were her contemporaries either have no descendants alive today, or are our ancestors through ancestral lines that include one or more males. This means that the mitochondrial DNA that is within every living human being is descended from the mitochondrial DNA that was within Mitochondrial Eve.

For Eve's mtDNA to be ancestral to all of the various mtDNA seen in the world today, it would mean that, over time, the mtDNA would need to have undergone a vast number of mutations. Because biologists have an idea of how quickly or slowly mtDNA mutates, we can estimate how far back in time Eve would have had to live in order for us to see the variation present in today's humans. Best estimates indicate that Eve lived about 200,000 years ago and, based on the distribution pattern of the mutations in the world, we can conclude that Eve lived somewhere in East Africa. Over time, some of Eve's female-line descendants spread out and were part of population migrations into the rest of Africa or into the Middle East, and from that area into Europe, Asia, Australasia, and the Americas.

Y-chromosomal Adam

Just as Mitochondrial Eve, living 200,000 years ago, can claim ancestry to all living humans through a direct female line, Y-chromosomal Adam (living at least as far back as 140,000 years ago and, according to some more recent studies, possibly more than 300,000 years ago) can claim ancestry to all living men through a direct male line. Again, Y-chromosomal Adam was not the only male in his population at the time he lived, but the other males either left no descendants alive today or have living descendants via lines that include one or more women. The Y-DNA found in every living human male is descended from Y-chromosomal Adam's Y-DNA, and the differences in that DNA found among living males is due to accumulated mutations over the many generations.

Haplogroups and SNPs

Throughout human pre-history and history, some human populations have stayed in one location for many generations, perhaps for thousands or tens of thousands of years. Some populations have split, leaving one group behind while another migrates to a new location. For most North Americans, we may think of our ethnic history as not where we live today (or even where our parents or grandparents have lived), and not where our human ancestors lived hundreds of thousands of years ago in East Africa, but instead during that vast time period in between, where our ancestors lived a few hundred or a few thousand years ago.

Because individuals in populations around the world have been tested for their mtDNA and their Y-DNA, biological and cultural anthropologists have been able to produce maps that indicate how human populations split off and migrated within and between continents in the pre-Columbian era. These maps are possible because specific mutations have been identified that are present in some populations but not in others.

At the beginning of this chapter's discussion of DNA, it was pointed out that the very long DNA molecule consists of a connected string of smaller molecules known as nucleotides, and each distinct type of nucleotide is identified by the abbreviations A, G, C, and T. If a mutation occurs during the DNA copying process where one of these nucleotides is replaced by a different nucleotide, it is known as a single nucleotide polymorphism (SNP, sometimes pronounced "snip"). When one of Mitochondrial Eve's daughters acquired this mutation while the other daughters did not, it meant that there were now two different groups of descendants: one group with the SNP, and one without. Mitochondrial Eve and any of her daughters who did not have the first SNP were assigned a group label of "L," while the descendant groups with mutations were given group labels that were either L followed by a number (L0, L1, L2, and so on) or a new letter (M, N, and so on). (See Figure 6-4.) These groups are known

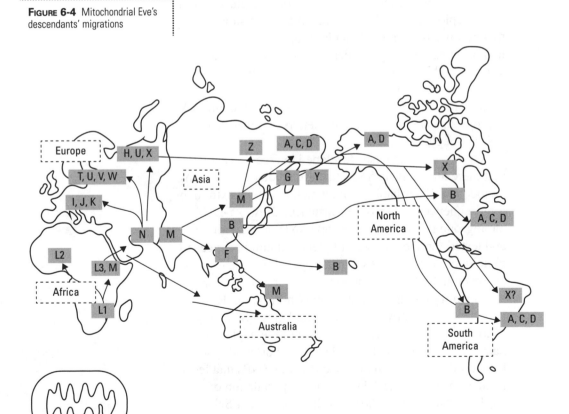

FIGURE 6-4 Mitochondrial Eve's descendants' migrations

as "haplogroups," meaning that everyone with the same SNP is part of a group of people descended from the first individual who had that SNP. Every human alive today can be assigned to a mitochondrial DNA haplogroup based upon which SNPs are found within their mtDNA. Once all of the letters (A–Z) were used to identify major haplogroups, numbers and lowercase letters were added to label subgroups. For instance, Drew's mtDNA haplogroup is identified as T2b13.

Just as the various descendant subgroups of Mitochondrial Eve can be assigned to haplogroups based upon the SNPs found in their mtDNA, the same can be done for the descendant subgroups of Y-chromosomal Adam. Over the generations, SNPs have accumulated in Y-DNA, and so letters, followed by a series of numbers and letters, are used to identify the various Y-chromosome DNA haplogroups. What you may find confusing is that because both mtDNA haplogroups and Y-DNA haplogroups use letters to identify the various groups, you might think that, for example, mtDNA Haplogroup A would have something to do with Y-DNA Haplogroup A. In reality, however, the letters assigned to the mtDNA haplogroups are unrelated to the letters assigned to the Y-DNA haplogroups.

One problem that has developed in recent years is that there are so many SNPs that are involved in defining a modern Y-DNA haplogroup, which results in extremely long sequences of labels. For instance, Drew's Y-DNA haplogroup is R1b1a2, but as new SNPs are identified and tested for, the number of letters and numbers needed to uniquely identify the subgroups gets longer and longer and eventually becomes unwieldy. A current solution is to identify the major haplogroup (in this case, R), and then follow it by the most recent known SNP (say, M269), creating a shorthand version of the haplogroup name (R-M269). The downside to the shorthand system is that it doesn't identify the sequence of SNPs that led from Y-chromosomal Adam to the subpopulation of modern descendants who carry the most recent SNP.

Ethnic Mixtures

By now, you may have figured out that a test of your mtDNA can identify a possible migration path that your maternal line took to get to you from Mitochondrial Eve in her African home. Drew's T mtDNA haplogroup is a likely indicator that Drew descends from Mitochondrial Eve through a series of women who migrated from Africa to Asia (around Syria or Turkey) to Europe (and eventually to the southern United States).

In the same way, Drew's R Y-DNA haplogroup, and more specifically R-M269, is extremely common in Ireland, which matches what Drew knows about his Smith ancestors. As shown in Figure 6-5, genetic maps can project the probable

FIGURE 6-5 Y-DNA migration map

migration paths that the paternal line took to get from Y-chromosomal Adam to Drew.

However, because the strictly maternal and strictly paternal lines represent only a tiny percentage of anyone's ancestral ethnicity, it is necessary to turn to autosomal DNA testing to get a more accurate picture. As mentioned before, if a distant ancestor came from a particular ethnic group, it is possible that no trace of that ancestor's DNA will be found in a living descendant. Drew's autosomal DNA test came back with an indicator that about 92.6 percent of his ancestry was Western European, and that the remaining percentage was South Asian (more specifically, North Indian or Southeast Indian). (See Figure 6-6.) The extremely large Western European percentage is not at all surprising, and the South Asian percentage may reflect ancestors who migrated several hundreds of years ago from India into the Middle East, the Mediterranean, or Eastern Europe. As you would expect, this kind of test might help to support (or refute) a claim that a particular ancestor was Native American or African American, but it cannot guarantee such results.

FIGURE 6-6 Family Finder— Population Finder

Companies That Perform DNA Testing

Once you have a general understanding of the types of DNA testing currently available, and the kinds of genealogical research questions that each can address, your next step is to understand which companies offer which kinds of tests, and what the pros and cons are of going with a particular company. Three companies have come to dominate the U.S. market in DNA testing for genealogical purposes: Family Tree DNA (http://www.familytreedna.com), 23andMe (https://www.23andme.com), and Ancestry.com (http://www.ancestry.com). Family Tree DNA was founded in 1999, while 23andMe was founded in 2006. Ancestry.com is better known for its online genealogical database subscription service, but it has entered the DNA market in recent years. All three of these companies offer an autosomal DNA test, and both Family Tree DNA and Ancestry.com offer tests specifically for either mtDNA or Y-DNA.

Because each company operates its own testing service and maintains its own online database of results, a test with one company will not automatically result in comparisons with customers who have chosen to test with a different company. Even worse, each company does not test the exact same set of markers as the other companies, so comparisons of results between companies is less effective than comparisons of results between individuals who tested with the same company.

Family Tree DNA is known for its active surname research groups, meaning that a Y-DNA test with Family Tree DNA may put the researcher in touch with a group of people sharing the same surname and provide a way to more easily determine which clusters of people with the same surname are actually related through that surname. 23andMe offers not only DNA testing for genealogy purposes but also for health purposes, although this may mean that DNA matches may not put you in contact with individuals who are interested in their family history. Ancestry.com is able to link its test results to its database of genealogical information. If cost is not a major concern, a researcher facing a brick wall situation may want to consider testing with more than one company in order to improve the chances of finding matching individuals.

It should be noted that each of these three companies periodically runs sales on their different testing services. Visit the sites often and watch the genealogy press for announcements of promotions and sales.

Specialized Genealogical Software

DNA testing is not the only recent technology intended to help genealogists get past their brick walls. In a previous chapter, we mentioned that it is important to make good use of one's genealogy database software. But you may not be aware of some software products that serve a different role in genealogical research. Let's look at three of these: GenSmarts, Clooz, and Evidentia.

GenSmarts

GenSmarts, a Windows-based software product, was first released in 2003, and is now in its second major version. Making use of a large database of known genealogical data repositories (primarily online sites, libraries, and archives) and their holdings, GenSmarts is able to analyze genealogical data for an individual or for a group of individuals, note what information is missing, and make recommendations as to where that information might be found. (See Figure 6-7.) The data for the individual of interest can be manually entered into GenSmarts, or GenSmarts can read the data directly from many popular genealogy software program databases or from any GEDCOM-format file. If you have GenSmarts already installed on your computer, you can even access its suggestions directly from current versions of RootsMagic (http://www.rootsmagic.com). GenSmarts can also assist you with cleaning up the place names in your data, asking you to provide missing county names for locations. Learn more about GenSmarts at http://www.gensmarts.com.

Depending upon how many different individuals you have GenSmarts analyze or how much information is missing for those individuals, GenSmarts may respond with hundreds or thousands of useful suggestions. These can be sorted by individual or by research repository, making it easier for you

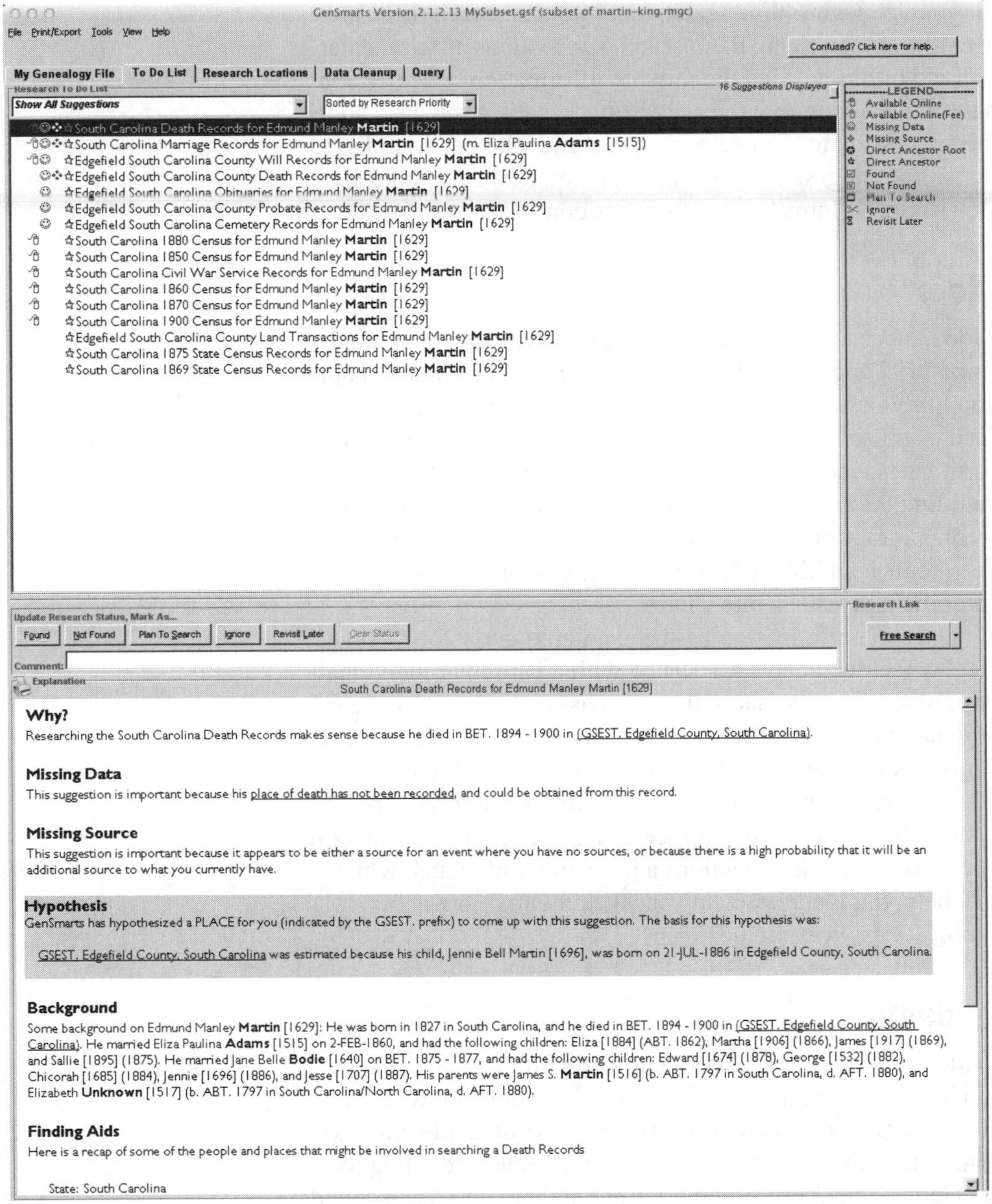

FIGURE 6-7 GenSmarts suggestions

to organize your online searching or your research trips. It also allows you to tag the research suggestions as to whether you did or did not find the missing information, whether you have chosen to ignore the suggestion, whether you have added the suggestion to your research plan, and whether you plan to revisit the suggestion at a later time. You can learn more about GenSmarts at http://www.gensmarts.com.

Clooz

Clooz, a Windows-based software product, has been around since 1997 and is now in its third major version. Clooz enables you to process a set of print documents or digital images, such as books, journal articles, census records, vital records certificates, and so forth, put them into a filing system, and then link them to the individuals whose names appear within them. Clooz works with any genealogy software program that can produce a GEDCOM-format file, or you can manually enter the individuals into Clooz.

Once the information has been entered into Clooz, you can display the documents associated with a particular individual, or produce a report that will show what documents you have or what your sources for those documents are. Clooz provides templates for common genealogy source types, making it easier to transcribe all of the key information into your filing system. In this way, you can see at a glance every document in your possession that mentions a particular individual, which will help you locate gaps in your files. Learn more about Clooz at http://www.clooz.com.

Evidentia

Evidentia, shown in Figure 6-8, available for both Windows and Mac systems, is a brand-new product, only a few months old at the time of this writing. The purpose of Evidentia is to help you analyze the evidence you have found according to the Genealogical Proof Standard, and to help you reach sound conclusions regarding that evidence. Because Evidentia is focused on your available sources, the information you find

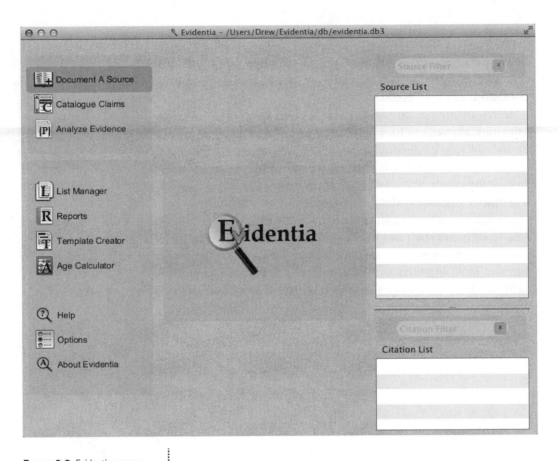

FIGURE 6-8 Evidentia screen

in those sources and the evidence that you derive from that information, you're in a better position to see whether you have good evidence that all points to the same conclusion or, instead, conflicting evidence that you will need to analyze and resolve. Once you have gone through this process, you will have a textual argument that you can copy into your genealogy software's notes section or that you can copy onto a website to showcase your research practices. Because Evidence is intentionally structured to use best genealogical practices, you are more likely to feel confident that you are making the best possible efforts to solve your brick wall problems. Learn more about Evidentia at http://evidentiasoftware.com.

Summary

By using both sound genealogical practices and the latest proven technologies, genealogists can have a better chance at getting past their brick wall problems.

DNA testing has already proven itself as a valuable genealogical research tool by providing evidence that either supports or refutes document-based conclusions, or by linking to otherwise unknown relatives, which may lead you to locate the missing paper pathway.

Popular genealogy database programs aren't the only way in which software can augment your research process. Unique software such as GenSmarts, Clooz, and Evidentia can address the specific research problems of identifying new places to look, organizing the documents already found, and highlighting the evidence for purposes of further analysis.

7

Hire a Demolition Expert

No one can be an expert in everything. As you walk through the forbidding forest and encounter a difficult barrier, it is quite acceptable to think to yourself, "I lack the knowledge and skills to get past this wall." You could return home, check the online professional directories for "Brick Wall Demolition Expert," and, after deciding which one to hire, turn your problem over to that person for a solution.

It is no different in the world of genealogical research. Your brick wall problem can often benefit from some professional help. So what might stop you from hiring a professional genealogical researcher?

Perhaps you think that it would take the fun out of doing research. Most of us are motivated to engage in researching our family trees because we enjoy solving the puzzles. We don't hire people to solve the Sunday newspaper crossword puzzle for us, do we? But let's assume that you've attempted to put into practice all of the other ideas already covered in this book, and nothing seems to be working. Is it all that much fun to keep banging your head against a problem that you can't seem to solve? If a professional researcher can get past your brick wall, you may find yourself once again in a position to solve the easier genealogical puzzles involved to extend your research on that target subject.

Perhaps you're worried that the next time you run into this kind of problem, you'll have to hire a researcher again. But part of a typical researcher's service is to provide the customer with a detailed report outlining what was searched, what was found, and what was concluded. Reading the professional's report can give you ideas on how you can approach future research problems.

Perhaps you're worried about the cost. But doing it yourself could be even more expensive. Imagine, instead of hiring a researcher who lives in the area where the records that apply to your brick wall problem are stored, you choose to travel to the location yourself. The cost of transportation, housing, and other expenses could easily far outstrip the cost of hiring someone who is already there and who already knows the geography and the available records.

Perhaps you're worried that you'll hire someone who is unskilled or unreliable. But we face this kind of problem whenever we hire professionals for the things we need. What do you do when you choose a doctor, an attorney, an accountant, a landscaper, or a housecleaning service? First, you depend on professional organizations that provide forms of accreditation. Doctors have to be licensed to practice in your state, and attorneys have to have passed a bar exam. No matter the type of professional, you consult online directories for details, you ask friends for their recommendations, and you go online to read reviews. The same kinds of things can be done in terms of hiring a genealogical professional.

What Can a Professional Researcher Do for Me?

A professional researcher can potentially advance your genealogy and, in doing so, overcome brick wall problems that you may have been unable to solve on your own. It is important to understand that people who want to accept clients and provide genealogical research services come in several varieties.

Professional Genealogist

A professional genealogist is one who has the knowledge and experience with accepted genealogical research methodologies and techniques, is familiar with a wide variety of genealogical record types, and has conducted research in many environments. They also have experience working with clients and producing concise reports on their findings on a timely basis. A person who uses the title "professional genealogist" may or may not be certified or accredited by a standards body.

There are other people who are experts in assisting in the creation of successful applications for heritage and lineage associations. They are usually members of these organizations themselves and have successfully helped other people compile the appropriate documentation and complete the applications.

Other people may be conversant in legal matters and documentation, and they can be invaluable in conducting research into estates, inheritances, and missing heirs.

They may be qualified and have the experience necessary to work with the legal system to research adoption cases.

You will need to evaluate the type(s) of research you need and to screen the professionals to locate the right person for the job.

Accredited Genealogist

The term Accredited Genealogist (AG) originated with the Church of Jesus Christ of Latter-day Saints. The International Commission for the Accreditation of Professional Genealogists, internationally recognized as ICAPGen (http://www.icapgen .org), now administers this organization, and its board of commissioners has many years of professional experience. (See Figure 7-1.)

ICAPGen offers accreditation in many different U.S. and international regions. Examinations are given to applicants to verify that they have sufficient theoretical and practical research backgrounds. A different exam is given for each geographical region, so that individuals who pass the exam are rightfully designated as research experts in that region. Exams may also include subjects of specialization. A successful individual is accredited for a period of five years, after which

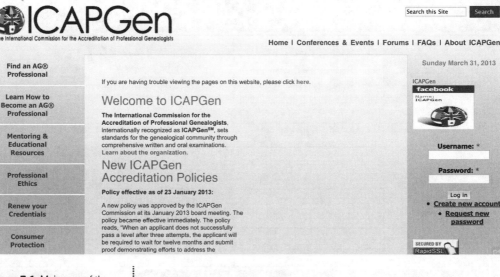

Figure 7-1 Main page of the ICAPGen website

time he or she may apply to renew the accreditation. Each AG is must adhere to a code of professional ethics. The person may use the credential of Accredited Genealogist in a resume and may use the postnominal of AG after their name in professional situations.

The ICAPGen website offers a search facility to locate a professional researcher by name, location, area of specialization, language proficiency, and other criteria.

Certified Genealogist

The Board for Certification of Genealogists, also referred to as BCG (http://www.bcgcertification.org), was begun in 1964 "to foster public confidence in genealogy as a respected branch of history by promoting an attainable, uniform standard of competence and ethics among genealogical practitioners, and by publicly recognizing persons who meet that standard." (See Figure 7-2.)

FIGURE 7-2 Main page of the Board for Certification of Genealogists website

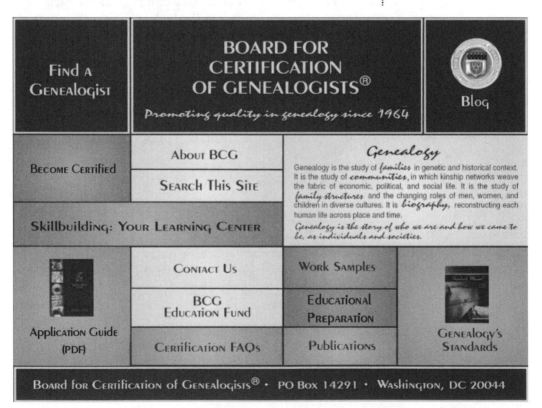

BCG is a certifying body that evaluates portfolios of research work samples submitted by applicants wishing to attain the credential of Certified Genealogist. Applications for certification are judged on whether they meet the standards delineated in the *BCG Genealogical Standards Manual,* published in 2000. Its standards contribute to the level of credibility in genealogy referred to as the Genealogical Proof Standard (GPS). As a result, genealogists who are certified have demonstrated their ability to do work that meets the GPS.

The organization offers two categories of certification, one of which is the Certified Genealogist. This category requires submission of detailed research work, documentation, and client research reports. The postnominal of CG is available for use by this individual.

Certified Genealogical Lecturer is the second category. It is an extension of the CG, and is the BCG teaching certification. The applicant provides detailed materials relating to two genealogical presentations, including digital audio or video copies, for evaluation. The postnominal of CGL is available for use by this individual.

BCG certification for the CG category is for five years, after which the certified individual must apply to renew the certification. The CGL certification coincides with the individual's CG certification. It, too, must be renewed at the conclusion of the CG five-year period. Each Certified Genealogist must adhere to a code of professional ethics.

The BCG website offers a search facility to locate a professional researcher by name, location, area of specialization, language proficiency, and other criteria.

Other Organizations Representing Professional Genealogists

Both ICAPGen and BCG are based in the United States, but the people holding credentials from those bodies represent research expertise in many areas of the world. There are also credentialing organizations in other parts of the world. These include the Association of Professional Genealogists in Ireland (APGI) (http://www.apgi.ie), the Association of Genealogists and Researchers in Archives (AGRA) (http://www.agra.org.uk), the Association of Scottish Genealogists and Researchers in Archives (http://www.asgra.co.uk), the Australasian Association of Genealogists and Record Agents, Inc. (http://www.aagra.asn .au), the Society of Australian Genealogists (SAG) (http://www .sag.org.au), the Genealogical Institute of the Maritimes (http:// nsgna.ednet.ns.ca/gim/), and the Union Chamber of Genealogy and Heraldry of France (http://www.csghf.org), among others.

The Association of Professional Genealogists (APG) (http:// www.apgen.org) is "an international organization dedicated to supporting those engaged in the business of genealogy through advocacy, collaboration, education, and the promotion of high ethical standards." It is not a certification body, but its members ascribe to a Code of Ethics. (See Figure 7-3.) The organization monitors compliance and disciplines any members against whom complaints have been received and who are found to have violated that code.

Professional genealogical researchers who have been certified or accredited have been tested on their research skills in specific areas and have produced satisfactory results as judged by a group of other professionals. Remember that

FIGURE 7-3 Association of Professional Genealogists web page

no single professional is skilled in every area of genealogical competence. For example, one researcher may focus on a particular geographical area while another may specialize in a particular set of records. The sections that follow explore some areas of specialty that you will want to consider as you search for a professional genealogical researcher to help solve your brick walls.

Geographic Specialization

A professional researcher will commonly indicate that he or she specializes in a specific geographical area and has extensive experience. You will be interested in reviewing which researchers work with records from the specific area where your ancestors lived or from which your ancestors migrated. This will be true either if you don't have the expertise to conduct effective research in that area, or if you don't want to personally travel to the area.

Perhaps your ancestors emigrated from a foreign country whose language you don't speak or read. Your European, Middle Eastern, or Asian ancestors' language may present a seemingly insurmountable roadblock for you. Your Canadian ancestor may have lived in an area where French was the official language. Official documents in England and Wales from the 1800s and before were created and maintained by ecclesiastics, and they were written in Latin. Documents for your Jewish ancestor may have been written in Hebrew or Yiddish, and stored in a synagogue under a person's Hebrew name. Even if you do speak the language of your ancestors, you may not be familiar with the vocabulary, culture, or handwriting styles of their time period.

In addition, the types of records that may have been created in other countries may be quite different from the American records you have used. In that case, a professional researcher who perhaps lives in that area and who is familiar with the records and the repositories where they are found would be a great help to your research. The researcher can identify where to seek records for your ancestors, visit or otherwise acquire copies, read and interpret the information, provide translations of the information, and evaluate the evidence in the correct geographical and historical context. The professional will produce a written report for you and provide copies of the materials located.

Specialty Areas

There are a multitude of specialties that professional researchers can provide. The following list, while not exhaustive, provides a strong representation of the geographies and/or record types in which professionals might specialize. Many professionals have experience in *multiple* research areas.

- Specific centuries, from the sixteenth to the twenty-first century
- Acadian research
- Adoption research
- African-American
- American Revolution
- Australia and New Zealand research
- Cajun research
- Canadian records—subsets include English and French records
- Caribbean research
- Catholic records
- Cemeteries
- Cherokee research
- Chinese research
- Choctaw research
- Church records
- Civil War
- Colonial United States
- Court records—subsets include federal, criminal, family court, probate, and other court records
- Cuban research
- Czech and Slovak research

- Daughters of the American Revolution
- Divorce research
- DNA and genetic genealogy
- English and Welsh research
- English manorial records
- Emigration records
- European research—subsets include various countries, past and present
- Federal records
- Five Civilized Tribes
- Freedmen research
- Genetic genealogy research (DNA)
- German research
- German-American
- German immigration records
- Heir searches
- Heraldry and Coats of Arms
- Hispanic research
- Historic houses and property research
- Holocaust research
- Huguenot research
- Immigration records (ships' passenger lists)
- Irish research
- Irish-American
- Irish immigration records
- Italian research
- Italian-American
- Italian immigration records
- Jamestown lineages
- Jewish—subsets include Ashkenazi, Sephardic, and other documentation

- Land platting
- Land and property records—subsets include State–Land State records, Federal Land records, Land Patents, Homestead records, and others
- LDS research
- Lineage society applications
- Mayflower lineages
- Mennonite research
- Military records—subsets include military service and pension records, various U.S. eras
- Native American—subsets include specific tribes and geographical areas
- Naturalization records
- Norwegian research
- Palatinate
- Palatine research
- Palatine immigrants
- Polish research
- Protestant religious groups
- Quaker research
- Scotland research
- Scotch-Irish research
- Scotch-Irish immigration
- Sons of the American Revolution
- Sons of the Confederacy
- Swedish research
- Russian research
- United Daughters of the Confederacy
- U.S. States research (individual and regional)
- World War I military records
- World War II military records

Contracting with a Professional Researcher

A professional researcher should always be willing to provide evidence of his or her credentials or proficiencies. That should include evidence of accreditation or certification, information about other professional organizations related to genealogy to which he or she belongs, and/or certificates or other proof of educational accomplishment. Remember that numerous professional researchers may not have sought certification, and that many of these are highly experienced and capable candidates to assist in your brick wall research. Some of the educational institutions that award educational certificates include:

- Brigham Young University
- Boston University
- Samford University's Institute of Genealogy and Historical Research (IGHR)
- National Institute on Genealogical Research (NIGR)
- National Institute for Genealogical Studies

Request client references from your researcher candidates, and follow through by contacting each person. Ask about the quality of the research that was conducted, the responsiveness of the researcher, and the overall experience.

Your relationship with a professional researcher should be formalized with a written contract. This sets forth the terms of the relationship and the deliverables, and protects both of you in the event of a conflict. A good contract will cover specifics:

- The goals of the research—What is/are the question(s) you want answered for what person(s)?
- What have you already researched? You don't want to pay a researcher to duplicate your research unless, of course, you both believe that the professional should reexamine the evidence.

■ What is the scope of the research? What geographical area, time period, record types, and document repositories should be included?

■ What are the researcher's fees?

■ What will you pay? Does that include travel, lodging, meals, document copies and photocopies, and other expenses? Will you be invoiced in increments and, if so, what are the measurable milestones? Will you be invoiced instead at the conclusion of the research and on receipt of a final report?

■ How will approval of additional expenses be handled?

■ Does the researcher plan to subcontract any of the work, especially in cases where the subcontractor has unique skills involving records in a particular language or in a particular geographic area where it would be too expensive for the researcher to travel? If so, how will you be able to judge the subcontractor's qualifications?

■ How often will you receive status reports and in what format?

■ What is the final deliverable that you want? This will typically consist of a client report describing all the research conducted, including information and evidence located *and not located,* copies of all documents, and complete source citations. A final, detailed accounting should also be requested.

If you have never hired a professional before, you may be unsure as to how much work you can expect for the fee you are willing to pay. It is a good idea to talk to others who have hired researchers so that you can set reasonable expectations. You can also expect that fees are going to differ depending upon the researcher's qualifications and experience. You may think that you will save money with a less experienced researcher, but keep in mind that the less experienced researcher may take longer to do the work than a more experienced researcher can do. When you're paying by the hour, you may not therefore be getting a bargain.

Another good idea when working with a professional for the first time is to contract for a relatively simple, inexpensive service, so that you can get an idea of the quality of the researcher's work and you can decide if you want to contract with them again to do more extensive work. In this way, you're not risking much the first time.

You and the professional should each sign and date the contract in the presence of witnesses or, if you are geographically distant from one another, each of you should sign in the presence of a notary public. Each of you should have a signed copy of the contract in hand before any work begins. If you later decide to modify the contract, such as to change the schedule of work done, the amount of work done, or the amount to be paid for the services, be sure to get those changes in writing, at the very least in e-mail form.

Cyndi's List has a collection of links to good resources describing when and how to engage the services of a professional researcher. Visit http://www.cyndislist.com/professionals/hiring to access and read these materials.

If and When Things Go Wrong

Let's assume, for the sake of argument, that you have hired a professional genealogist, specifically one who is a member of the Association of Professional Genealogists, and things haven't worked out quite as you expected. First, let's be clear that we don't mean that the professional genealogist didn't solve your brick wall problem. There are no guarantees here, and if the professional actually made such a guarantee, you weren't dealing with a true professional. And second, let's be just as clear that the vast majority of professionals do not disappoint their clients with the work that they do.

When we talk about a professional not meeting expectations, we mean that they didn't honor the contract by providing the services that were contracted for at the agreed upon price in a timely manner. When there are complaints about the work of professional genealogists, those complaints are normally about the professional not communicating in a reasonable manner with the client, or not providing the promised report in the expected format or according to the expected schedule.

Clearly, your first step is to make a serious attempt to work things out with the professional. It is certainly possible that the professional was delayed by a personal problem, such as a health-related issue or a family emergency. It is also entirely possible that the professional underestimated the amount of work involved or the amount of time needed to produce the expected results. In these cases, your best course of action is to attempt to renegotiate the contract so that both sides get what they want.

But sometimes your best efforts still don't result in a reasonable response from the professional. If this happens, and the professional is a member of APG, you can use APG's process for filing a complaint. In such cases, APG has a Professional Review Committee (PRC), which is charged with looking at any such complaints and addressing them according to standard procedures. There are some things that the PRC will not address. For instance, if your disagreement with the professional is based upon a verbal agreement and not a written one, then the PRC won't have any evidence to examine in order to render a decision. The PRC will need to see an agreement that was in writing, whether in a written contract, a letter, or an e-mail.

If your disagreement relates to something other than an agreement for some sort of genealogical services, or if the complaint is based upon something that happened more than a year before the time the complaint is filed, the PRC won't look at those either, so it is important not to wait too long if you plan to file a complaint.

If your complaint meets the criteria required by APG and the policies of the PRC, then you will be advised that the PRC will investigate the complaint, and APG will advise the member who is the subject of the complaint so that they can make a written response and provide whatever evidence that they feel is relevant. This material will also be forwarded to the PRC so that the PRC can examine both sides of the issue.

In many cases, the very fact of having a complaint filed against them will result in the member's quickly making good on whatever the problem was, and in such cases, the case may be closed. Ideally, APG wants the professional and the client to work out their issues without the need for any official action taken by APG against its member. However, in some cases, when these situations are not resolved between the professional and the client, any of several results may occur. The PRC will make a recommendation to the leadership of APG regarding the complaint, and the leadership of APG will make a final decision as to how to handle the situation. APG may come down on the side of the complainant, and instruct the member as to what they should do in order to rectify the situation. If the complaint is sufficiently serious, APG may suspend the professional's membership in APG for a period of time (one or more years), or may permanently expel the member.

In other cases, APG may reject the claim because it decides that the member did not violate the contract, or that the complainant hasn't provided sufficient evidence to show that the contract was violated. In some cases, no conclusion will be reached, usually due to a lack of sufficient evidence to make a decision.

If the professional you hired is certified by ICAPGen, BCG, or another certifying body, you will want to make certain to contact the respective body to apprise them of your experience.

It should be noted that APG cannot address complaints against professional genealogists who are not members of APG, and in any case, complaints represent a very tiny percentage of all transactions between professionals and clients. Even so, it is nice to know that there are methods of recourse if the terms of a contract are not met. Professional genealogists depend very much on having an excellent reputation, and nearly all will make every effort to deal honestly and appropriately with their clients.

Summary

It's not always possible to do your own genealogical research. The reasons can be numerous. Sometimes it isn't logistically or financially possible to make a trip to the locations where your ancestors lived.

You may not have the knowledge and experience to locate the evidence and to prove facts to justify your hypotheses. Your inability to understand the language in which the records were written or to decipher the handwriting or script used at the time the records were created may be major stumbling blocks.

Whatever the reasons, it may be more practical to engage a professional researcher to help you get past your brick walls. He or she may be the demolition expert you need to use. Each type of researcher we've discussed in this chapter will need to possess appropriate credentials and references. Your job is to conduct an interview and investigation process to make sure you have the right person with the appropriate experience and credentials to successfully conduct research on your behalf.

8

Rest Up and Attack
the Brick Wall Another Time

You find yourself in that dense woods, facing the obstacle of a brick wall barring your path, and nothing you have tried has gotten you past it. You've examined each brick carefully; you've used brute force; you've looked for ways around it; you've enlisted help from friends, the general public, and professionals; and you've used the latest wall-scaling technology. Nothing has worked. There is only one option left.

Give up.

But only for now.

In the real world of forests and walls, things change. Brick walls are eroded by the weather and by plants and animals, and new paths are laid in the forest. You might even return at a later date to find that someone else has built some steps or put a ladder up against the wall. It can be just a matter of time and patience.

If you're like most genealogists, you find that you don't make progress with your research in a constant manner. You make great progress for a while, and then the progress becomes more difficult. You may set aside your research in a particular ancestral line for a month, a year, or several years. When you return to it, it's not quite the same as it was when you left it.

In this chapter, we talk about the benefits of setting your brick wall problem aside, and what you can do productively during the time that you're not directly working on that problem.

Learn

We cannot remember a week going by when we weren't learning something new about doing genealogical research. The ways in which you can continue your education in genealogy include reading books, articles, blog postings, and wiki entries; listening to audio files and watching videos; attending genealogical society meetings; participating in one or more SIG meetings; attending live webinars and face-to-face presentations; or watching recorded and archived webinars.

Books

Over the years, we each have assembled a large personal library of some of the best genealogy how-to and methodology books ever written. Figure 8-1 shows a portion of Drew's library catalog on LibraryThing.com. Even the oldest books in the collection contain a great deal of wisdom regarding the practice of doing genealogical research, and the more recent books supplement the classics by providing ways to

FIGURE 8-1 LibraryThing showing a small portion of Drew's personal library

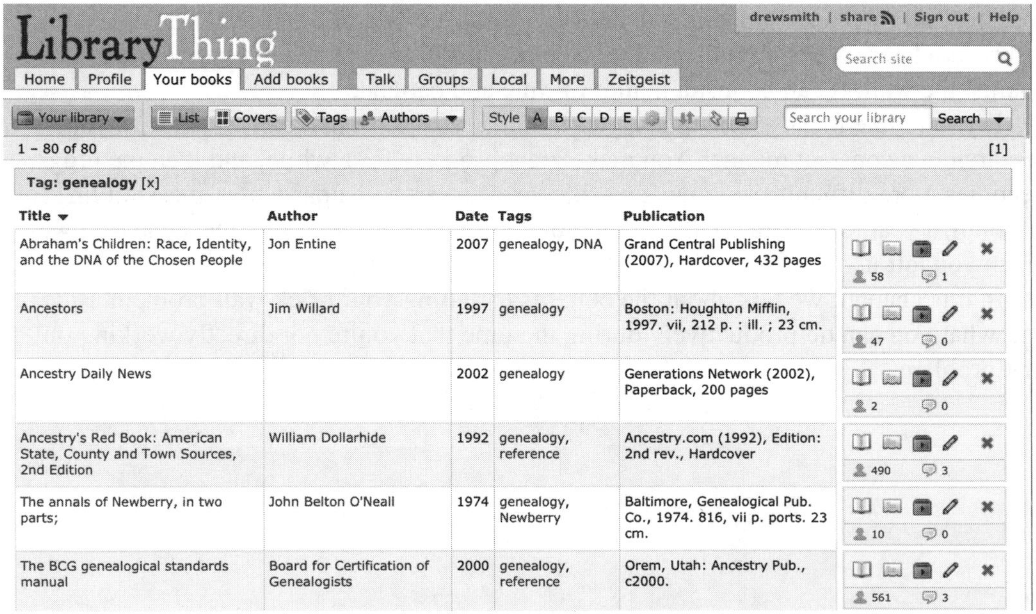

LibraryThing

drewsmith | share | Sign out | Help

Home | Profile | Your books | Add books | Talk | Groups | Local | More | Zeitgeist

Search site

Your library | List | Covers | Tags | Authors | Style A B C D E | Search your library | Search

1 – 80 of 80   [1]

Tag: genealogy [x]

Title ▼	Author	Date	Tags	Publication		
Abraham's Children: Race, Identity, and the DNA of the Chosen People	Jon Entine	2007	genealogy, DNA	Grand Central Publishing (2007), Hardcover, 432 pages	58 1	
Ancestors	Jim Willard	1997	genealogy	Boston: Houghton Mifflin, 1997. vii, 212 p. : ill. ; 23 cm.	47 0	
Ancestry Daily News		2002	genealogy	Generations Network (2002), Paperback, 200 pages	2 0	
Ancestry's Red Book: American State, County and Town Sources, 2nd Edition	William Dollarhide	1992	genealogy, reference	Ancestry.com (1992), Edition: 2nd rev., Hardcover	490 3	
The annals of Newberry, in two parts;	John Belton O'Neall	1974	genealogy, Newberry	Baltimore, Genealogical Pub. Co., 1974. 816, vii p. ports. 23 cm.	10 0	
The BCG genealogical standards manual	Board for Certification of Genealogists	2000	genealogy, reference	Orem, Utah: Ancestry Pub., c2000.	561 3	

apply those well-tested methods using the latest technology. These books all refer to specific record types and discuss their content and how to effectively analyze and document them.

As part of your own personal library, look for books that discuss the methods and records pertaining to a particular ethnic group or geographical area. Although some genealogical research methods are universal, some work better than others when you're dealing with differing cultures and the kinds of records they leave behind. You might begin the development of your personal collection by looking for books still in print, which you can obtain either through a general online bookseller (Amazon.com, for instance) or through an online genealogy bookseller. If you attend a national, state, or large local genealogy conference, visit the vendor exhibit hall for the booths that sell books, and let the salesperson know the kinds of books you are looking for. Sellers may not have brought their entire inventory to the conference, but they can often recommend other titles that you can order from their catalog or that may be carried by a different vendor.

When buying a new genealogical methodology book, look to see if the book can be purchased as an e-book, as this means you'll be able to carry it around with you on a tablet device and learn from it when you're traveling or killing time in a waiting room.

Although the best methodology books tend to stay in print, books that cover records for a particular area may be harder to find. The first trick is to identify the titles and authors of useful books. In the past, you would normally need to do separate searches of the FamilySearch Library catalog (https://www .familysearch.org/catalog-search) and the OCLC WorldCat library catalog (http://www.worldcat.org) in order to do a reasonably comprehensive search for genealogy-related books, but in February 2013, FamilySearch and OCLC announced that the FamilySearch catalog records would be added to WorldCat in the near future. Once you have used these library catalogs to figure out which books might be of the most value to your personal library collection, you can then look to see if each book has been scanned and made available online or if the book would need to be purchased in print format. If you want a copy of an out-of-print book for your personal library,

there are many online used-book seller websites including
AddALL (http://www.addall.com), Bookfinder (http://www
.bookfinder.com), and viaLibri (http://www.vialibri.net).
Check those to see if anyone is selling a used copy of the
book. Figures 8-2 and 8-3 show the main webpages of AddAll
and viaLibri.

Articles

A number of popular genealogy magazines and society
journals exist that bring a printed copy to your postal
box (or, increasingly, a digital copy to your computer
or handheld device) of some of the best techniques for
engaging in research. Each issue may provide an idea that
had never previously occurred to you, something that you
can try with your own brick walls. North American–based

FIGURE 8-2 The results of
a search of AddALL for used
genealogy how-to books

Find Ebooks? Try AddALL Ebooks!!

| Memo | Saved Search | Contact us | Customize view | Search New Books | Help |
[**Search Again:** Blank new search | Keep last search terms]

Printer friendly | Save this search | Search for ", genealogy how to" at eBay

Our search for Keyword: **genealogy how to**, brought up 371 title(s). Sorting by **Price Ascending**.
CLICK HERE to change your search preferences

Result in pages: 1 - 2 - 3 - 4 - 5 - 6 - 7 - 8 - ▶
Please add our search engine to your site. Get the codes here.
Use this url to pass this search result on to a friend:
Page id: http://used.addall.com/SuperRare/RefineRare.fcgi?id=130413161201561246

Save the Info	Sort Asc **TITLE** Sort Desc *Click on the link for more info*	**Asc AUTHOR Desc**	**Asc PRICE USD Desc**	**Asc SITE Desc**	**Asc DEALER Desc**	**DESCRIPTION**
save	1 **Searching for Your Ancestors: the How and Why of Genealogy**[Buy it!] [show this book only]	Doane, Gilbert H.; Bell, James B.	0.99	Alibris	Crazy Ladies Bookshop via Alibris	Chicago, Illinois, U.S.A. Univ of Minnesota Pr 1992 6th ed. Trade Paper Good Used Good condition. Tradepaper. Used. Cover good. Pages tight and clean.
save	2 **Searching for Your Ancestors: How and Why of Genealogy**[Buy it!] [show this book only]	Gilbert H. Doane, James B. Bell	0.99	Alibris	Green Earth Books via Alibris	University of Minnesota Press 1980 5th ed. Hardcover Fine Almost in new condition. Book shows only very slight signs of use. Cover and binding are undamaged and pages show minimal use.

| Home | Wants Manager | Libribot | Libraries | Links | 557 Years | More | 🇬🇧 ▮▮ ▬ | Login / Register |

*via*Libri
Digital Tools For Bibliophiles

The World's Largest Marketplace for Old, Rare & Out-of-print Books

First 302 viaLibri Matches For: Author: = , Title: , Imprint: = , Keyword: = **genealogy how-to**, [Prices are Rounded]

New Search	Page: **1** (of 7) ▷

Edit Search

Sort again by...
Price ⌄
Ascending ⌄
Sort Now

☐ **Remove** [# 1]   ⌄⌃ ⌄⌃   Translate

Barbara Howell
How to Trace Your African-American Roots: Discovering Your Unique History
Citadel 2000. , Very good
[Bookseller : *Sierra Nevada Books*]

Buy From: Alibris $ 1   Clipboard

☐ **Remove** [# 2]   ⌄⌃ ⌄⌃   Translate

Barbara Howell
How to Trace Your African-American Roots: Discovering Your Unique History
Citadel 2000. This copy shows very minor wear. Free State Books. Never settle for less , Very good
[Bookseller : *Free State Books*]

Buy From: Alibris $1   Clipboard

FIGURE 8-3 The results of a search of viaLibri for used genealogy how-to books

popular magazines include *Family Tree Magazine* (see Figure 8-4), published by F+W Media; *Family Chronicle* and *Internet Genealogy* (see Figures 8-5 and 8-6), published by Moorshead Magazines; and *FGS FORUM* (see Figure 8-7) published by the Federation of Genealogical Societies. A number of national genealogy societies publish magazines as a benefit of membership, including the *NGS Magazine,* published by the National Genealogical Society (NGS), and *American Ancestors,* published by the New England Historic Genealogical Society (NEHGS). Many state and local genealogy societies publish newsletters that discuss specific research methods and local record collections.

Beyond the general how-to articles that appear in the previously mentioned magazine-style publications, a number of societies produce quarterly journals, usually available as part of society membership. These journals specialize in providing examples of the best practices in genealogical research, and reading these journals represents one of the best ways you can take your own research skills to a higher level.

FIGURE 8-4 Family Tree Magazine

FIGURE 8-5 Family Chronicle

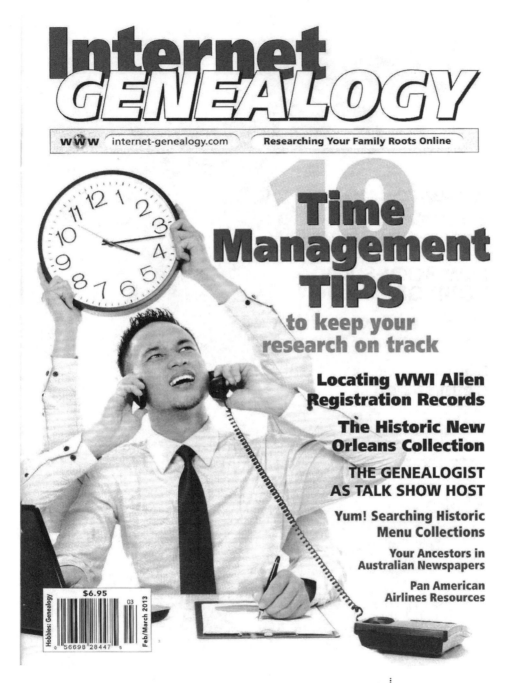

FIGURE 8-6 Internet Genealogy

FIGURE 8-7 The FGS FORUM

Examples include the *NGS Quarterly* (NGSQ) (see Figure 8-8), published by the National Genealogical Society, and the *New England Historical and Genealogical Register,* published by the New England Historic Genealogical Society.

But what of all the articles that may have appeared in a genealogy magazine, newsletter, or journal in the past 200 years? Fortunately, you can use the PERiodical Source Index (PERSI), an online database published by the Allen County (IN) Public Library (ACPL), to discover articles written on specific methodologies or about specific places. PERSI is available in two ways: It is available to Ancestry.com home subscribers (it is not part of the Ancestry Library Edition, available for use in some public libraries), and it is part of the HeritageQuest Online product offered by ProQuest. If you do not subscribe to Ancestry.com, check with your public library to see whether it offers HeritageQuest Online and, if it does, whether you can access it from home. Figures 8-9 and 8-10 show screen images from HeritageQuest Online.

Once you have located a relevant article, you can check with your local public library to see if they have a copy of the issue in which the article appeared, or whether the library can obtain a copy for you using interlibrary loan (ILL). If ILL is not an option, you can request the article directly from ACPL for a small fee. Once you have obtained a copy of a useful article, you can scan it into digital form and save a copy on your home computer for future reference. You might even save the digital copy into your genealogy database program as a media item for the person(s) for whom the article's contents apply.

National Genealogical Society Quarterly

Volume 99, No. 2, June 2011

FIGURE 8-8 The NGS Quarterly

FIGURE 8-9 The PERSI How To search template

HERITAGE QUEST ONLINE

| CENSUS | BOOKS | PERSI | FREEDMAN'S | REV WAR | SERIA |

People :: Places :: How To's :: Periodicals

How To's

Search for articles about research methodologies.

To search the PERiodical Source Index, provide any of the following criteria and click the search button:

Keywords   immigration   Examples: Colonial, Finding, Ohio
Record Type [All   ‡]

[SEARCH ►]
[CLEAR SEARCH]

HERITAGE QUEST ONLINE

| CENSUS | BOOKS | PERSI | FREEDMAN'S | REV WAR | SERIA |

People :: Places :: How To's :: Periodicals

Article Results List   Refine

334 of 334 results for Keywords: immigration

Page 1 of 7   1 2 3 4 5 6 7

1. ☐ Tips on German Gothic script, boundaries, territories, and immigration research
       German Interest Group Newsletter. Janesville WI: Aug 2009. Vol. 16 Iss. 2

2. ☐ How to use the New York Times interactive immigration map
       Germanic Genealogy Journal. St. Paul MN: Summer 2009. Vol. 12 Iss. 2

3. ☐ Immigration A-files description, preservation, and access notes, 1907+
       Ventura County Genealogical Society Newsletter. Ventura CA: Jul 2009. Vol. 32 Iss. 7

4. ☐ Websites to find your family's past immigration history
       Galizien German Descendants. Walnut Creek CA: Jul 2009. Vol. - Iss. 59

5. ☐ Timeline of United States immigration laws, 1790-2003
       Suncoast Searcher. Crystal Beach FL: Jun 2009. Vol. 26 Iss. 6

FIGURE 8-10 PERSI search results

Blogs

Many experienced genealogists maintain blogs, even when they are already writing books and articles for periodicals. These blogs are free to read and contain a treasure trove of tips and techniques relating to genealogical methods and resources. To locate a blog that may relate directly to your ethnic or geographical area of interest, use one of the two major genealogy blog directories: Chris Dunham's *Genealogy Blog Finder* (http:// blogfinder.genealogue.com), shown in Figure 8-11, or Thomas MacEntee's *Geneabloggers* (http://geneabloggers.com), shown in Figure 8-12. You can also use the directories to search for specific blog postings that may be relevant to your research, and you can subscribe to the directories to get updates when new blogs are added to the directories.

If you find a particular blog useful, you will probably want to subscribe to it using the RSS feed option (this option may appear as a small orange square or rectangle on the blog's home page). You can use a web-based feed reading service,

FIGURE 8-11 Genealogy Blog Finder

which is normally free, in order to keep on top of a number of different blogs of interest.

You may want to download and save copies of especially useful blog postings so that you can refer to them even when you're not online (and so that you have the information even if the original author removes the posting or experiences technical problems with the blog).

Wikis

Over the past few years, two significant genealogy wikis have come into existence, providing an encyclopedic-style reference resource for describing research methods and for identifying key resources for specific ethnic groups and geographic areas. The FamilySearch Research Wiki (https://www.familysearch .org/learn/wiki/en/Main_Page), shown in Figure 8-13, and the Ancestry.com Family History Wiki (http://www.ancestry .com/wiki/index.php?title=Main_Page), shown in Figure 8-14, are valuable free resources that you can consult for constantly updated information about research techniques and record

GeneaBloggers
The ultimate site for your genealogy blog

Search

Home   About   FAQs   Blogging Resources   Daily Blogging Prompts   Genealogy Blog Roll   **Genealogy Blogs By Type**

Search Blogs   Suggest A Blog

Genealogy Blogs By Type

A new feature at GeneaBloggers is the ability to view groups of genealogy blogs and blog posts organized by type.

New genealogy blogs are assigned blog types based on a cursory review of blog content. *If you feel your blog has been assigned an incorrect type please e-mail* geneabloggers@gmail.com *to have it corrected.*

- Acadian Genealogy
- Afrikaans Genealogy
- African-American Genealogy
- Alabama Genealogy
- Appalachian Genealogy
- Argentina Genealogy
- Arizona Genealogy

FIGURE 8-12 Genealogy Blogs by Type at GeneaBloggers.com

collections. By reviewing these wiki articles, you will get a better understanding of resources that you can apply to your brick wall problems.

Recorded Audio and Video Programs

As transmission speeds have increased on the Internet, and consumers have shifted from slower dial-up connections to high-speed cable connections, it has become more feasible to transmit audio and video across the Web. We have been producing free hour-long audio programs since September 2005,

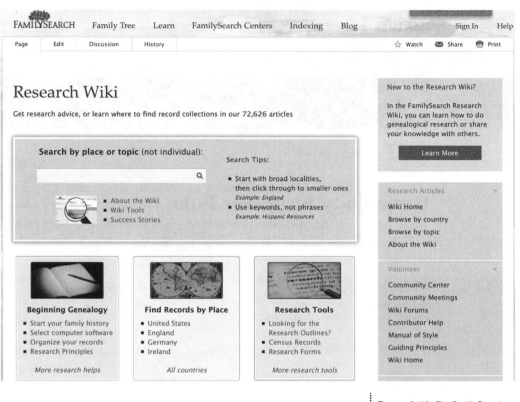

FIGURE 8-13 The FamilySearch Research Wiki

and now have well over 250 episodes of *The Genealogy Guys Podcast*, shown in Figure 8-15, for you to listen to at http://genealogyguys.com. Regular listeners often write to say that they have picked up a tip or technique from the programs, and listeners also e-mail the podcast to provide an idea for solving a particular research problem. Other podcasts, such as The Genealogy Gems Podcast (http://genealogygemspodcast.com), are also full of research ideas.

If you are looking for more structured programs, you might enjoy any of the hundreds of audio and video tutorials offered for free by FamilySearch in the Learning Center on their website (https://www.familysearch.org/learningcenter/home.html), shown in Figure 8-16. These recorded programs range from beginners' courses to courses designed around specific geographic areas or record types.

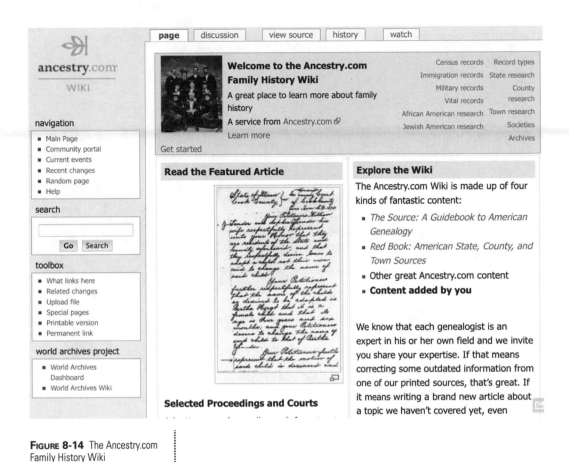

The Ancestry.com Family History Wiki

Several national organizations, such as the National Genealogical Society (NGS) and the Association of Professional Genealogists (APG), offer video tutorials to their members using the members-only sections of their websites.

Live Webinars

Another benefit from the faster Internet speeds comes in the form of the proliferation of genealogy webinars. These live presentations always involve at least audio of the presenter, together with a display of PowerPoint-style slides, and often with a live video feed so that you can see what the presenter looks like. In many cases, the webinars are free to the general

The Genealogy Guys Podcast

George G. Morgan and Drew Smith discuss genealogy. This is the longest-running, regularly produced genealogy podcast in the world!

Sun, 7 April 2013

 **The Genealogy Guys Podcast #249 – 2013 April 7**

George is out of town speaking for the North Carolina Genealogical Society, so Drew hosts this episode, beginning with the following news items:

- British Origins adds South London burials to its London collection.
- The Federation of Genealogical Societies (FGS) announces a new partnership with its German equivalent, the German Association of Genealogical Associations (DAGV).
- FamilySearch indexing volunteers reach the 1 billion record milestone.
- Houstory thanks The Genealogy Guys for their previous coverage of their Heirloom Registry product.
- Ancestry.co.uk adds Wiltshire Church Records and Wiltshire Quaker Birth & Death records to its collection.
- AncestryDNA makes it easier to communicate with people who match, improves its website for mobile users, and provides the ability to download raw DNA data.
- Tim Sullivan, CEO of Ancestry.com, makes several important announcements at RootsTech 2013, including the new partnership with FamilySearch to digitize 140 million pages of U.S. probate

The Genealogy Guys
Drew (l) and George (r)

Search

| | Search |

Contact Us

genealogyguys@gmail.com
Facebook
GenealogyWise
Google+

FIGURE 8-15 The Genealogy Guys Podcast

public, or are at least free to members of a sponsoring society; in other cases, there is a charge.

An advantage of attending a live webinar is that you may be able to ask questions of the presenter. This means that you may have yet another opportunity to put your brick wall problem in front of an expert, especially when your problem is related in some way to the topic of the webinar.

Many webinars are recorded and are available for later viewing. This is a great advantage in several ways. First, you can watch a webinar in the event that you couldn't fit it into your schedule when it was presented live. Second, you may not have been interested in the topic being presented at the time. It is great to be able to watch the presentation later when you want or need it.

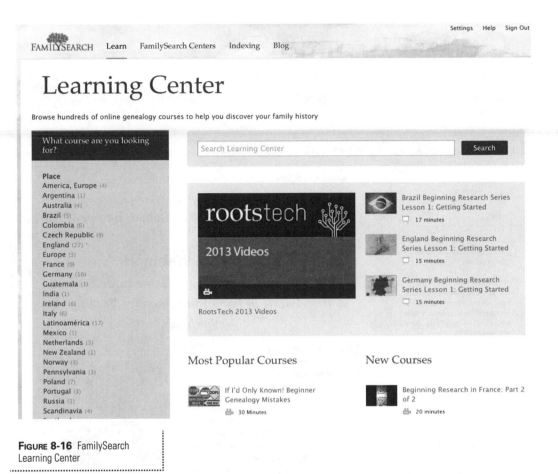

FIGURE 8-16 FamilySearch Learning Center

To find a comprehensive calendar of upcoming genealogy webinars, visit GeneaWebinars at http://geneawebinars.com shown in Figure 8-17.

Face-to-Face Presentations

Despite the fact that learning at home (or while traveling) from books, articles, blogs, wikis, audio and video programs, and webinars is extremely convenient, there is no perfect educational substitute for attending a face-to-face genealogy presentation. Whether it's an educational program offered by your local public library, by your local genealogy society as part of its monthly meeting, or an all-day seminar or multi-day conference sponsored by a local, state, or national

GeneaWebinars

News about upcoming hangouts, meetings and webinars offered throughout the online genealogy community.

Home	WELCOME	Calendar	How it works	Webinar Hosts	Virtual Speakers

WELCOME to GeneaWebinars - a group calendar and blog.

We provide information genealogy-related online meetings, classes, hangouts, seminars and webinars, where there is a visual slide share and/or website or software demo for attendees to view.

Hosts may use a variety of platforms including Adobe Connect, AnyMeeting, Captera, Google Hangouts, GoToMeeting, GoToWebinar, Live Meeting, Skype, Web-Ex, and Wiggio, to name a few.

There are currently over 35 with posting access to this calendar and blog, and over 200 hours of scheduled instruction for genealogists wishing to hone their research skills during the coming year. If you'd like to join the calendar to post your organization's events, just drop a note to Myrt@DearMYRTLE.com.

Thursday, April 11, 2013

Wooden Shoe Genealogy: Methods for Tracing North American Immigrant Families Back to The Netherlands

Join Us for Our April Webinar!

"Wooden Shoe Genealogy: Methods for Tracing North American Immigrant Families Back to The Netherlands"

Presenter: J. H. Fonkert
J. H. ("Jay") Fonkert is a genealogical researcher, writer and educator based in St. Paul, Minnesota. Past President of the Minnesota Genealogical Society, he is managing editor of Minnesota Genealogist. Jay's research interests extend from the American Midwest to The Netherlands, England and Scandinavia. His teaching articles have appeared in Minnesota Genealogist, The Septs, NGS Magazine and Family Chronicle, and his research has been published in the National Genealogical Society Quarterly.

Date: Tuesday, April 16th, 2013

FIGURE 8-17 GeneaWebinars

genealogical society, there are several aspects of face-to-face education that cannot truly be matched by the virtual variety.

Local genealogy societies have already been mentioned as a way to bring your brick wall problem in front of a supportive and helpful audience. During the social aspects before and after a face-to-face presentation, you may be talking to other genealogists about their own research issues, and their experiences may shed light on your own problem.

More to the point, the expert who is presenting as part of a face-to-face educational program may be available prior to the program to hear your question or, usually better for all concerned, you can ask your question during the question and answer portion of the session. At the end of the presentation, you may be able to talk individually with the presenter if he or she is free for a few minutes. At a multi-day conference, there may be experts present who are knowledgeable specifically about the types of records, the geographic areas, or the time periods relating to your brick wall problem. Experts may include presenters, representatives from societies or governmental organizations, and vendors of books, software, and a wide variety of services.

Your focus, however, does not have always have to be about your specific brick wall problem. No matter what type of presentation you attend, what you learn may turn out to have some kind of application to your own research, and you may suddenly make a connection between a technique that was presented to you and something that you can do to apply a similar technique to your own problem. This constitutes a type of "outside-the-box" approach to applying newly learned techniques to problems that don't initially appear to fit the technique.

Practice

No matter how much you learn from reading, listening to, and watching educational materials, you probably won't benefit from the new ideas until you put them into practice. There is no sharp dividing line between a beginning genealogist and an intermediate or advanced genealogist, and in reality, you may be a beginner in some areas of research and a more expert researcher in other areas. As you work on more and more of your own research, you will instinctively become a better researcher and you will develop good research habits as you apply the ideas you have learned from the experts in the field.

As you continue to practice your work, don't worry if you're not spending any time on a particular brick wall problem. The time you are spending working on other family lines may increase your experience level so that, when you do choose to return to that difficult problem, you may find that you are seeing it in a different way.

One way to improve your overall skill level is to work on a variety of problems. For instance, you might vary the geographic areas you are dealing with, or the time periods involved. You might switch from working backwards in time from a particular ancestor, and choose instead to work forwards in time from an immigrant ancestor to their descendants in a number of lines. Ideally, you will want to work with as many different record types as you can, to gain confidence in their use. Move beyond censuses, vital records, tombstones, and newspaper obituaries to include more challenging records, such as land and probate materials.

Monitor

One of the most exciting things about being a genealogist working in the twenty-first century is that the environment in which we work is constantly changing. While the physical materials we depend upon are still there, in their usual places in libraries, archives, courthouses, and cemeteries, we are seeing materials being digitized, placed online, and indexed at an increasingly faster rate. This means that the websites for FamilySearch, commercial genealogy services, government offices, and libraries and archives are constantly changing and becoming more and more valuable over time. As you can imagine, this suggests that a document key to solving your brick wall problem may appear online at any moment. You will need to go to these online sources on a regular basis to look for new collections or additions and corrections to existing collections to see if any of these changes are relevant to your research. You may want to set up a calendar for yourself with monthly reminders telling you which sites you should check and what searches to perform.

If you have previously turned up no useful results in genealogy mailing lists and message boards, you will need to remind yourself to also check those on a regular basis in the future because you never know when a new message might be posted by a new genealogist that relates to your brick wall problem. Some message boards allow you to monitor them for specific key words, sending an alert to your e-mail. Some of the online family tree sites also allow you to "watch" a particular ancestral individual to see if anyone else has added to or edited their information.

Summary

It may seem counterintuitive to walk away from a brick wall problem in order to solve it, but, in reality, it speaks to the fact that, given enough time, things change in important and significant ways. If you put your mind to it, you can change yourself as a genealogist, becoming better educated and more skilled with practice. And the environment in which you work will also change, as new record collections become part of searchable databases and new genealogists go online with their own knowledge and willingness to share and help. When you return to your brick wall problem, you may even look at it and wonder why it seemed so difficult before when it seems solvable now.

9

Put the Techniques to Work

We began this book with the intention of providing different methods of approaching the genealogical brick walls that we all encounter. Contemporary research involves a blend of many types of resources; some are old and familiar, while others are new to us. Let's begin our discussion in this chapter by saying that there is no shortcut in successful family history research. It is always necessary to identify the original documents and other sources, determine where they are located, and either examine them personally on-site or acquire exact images of them so that we can directly examine and evaluate them ourselves. Transcriptions, extracts, and abstracts are poor substitutes for the originals, as you've seen, and can often introduce errors. Published genealogies may also contain errors, and data that other researchers may have published in print or electronic format may create new errors and perpetuate other people's mistakes.

Review the Evidence

Evidence comes in many forms and formats, and it comes to you in no particular sequence. You analyze it as you acquire it, and draw hypotheses based on what you know at the time. You then perhaps enter it into a genealogy database *with source citations* and then set it aside. We discussed developing an ancestor profile, or timeline, in Chapter 4. During that process, you are forced to arrange all of the evidence for a particular person or family in chronological sequence. You can then reread each item and analyze it in geographical and chronological context, not unlike reading a biography. When you create the timeline, you see the person's life more clearly, identify gaps in our research, and assess the quality and strength of each piece of evidence. You may also discover conflicting evidence and missing source citations, all of which will need to be addressed.

It becomes clear when you reexamine the entire body of the evidence you have collected that you have more information than you thought you had. Pieces begin to fit together to present a more contextual picture. You also can better focus on the types of information from specific geographical areas and time periods that you want to find.

Develop a Research Strategy

Experienced genealogists know how important it is to develop a research strategy. This helps you set goals and maintain a focus, both of which are essential when working on a brick wall problem. Several steps are involved when you develop a plan for attacking your obstacle.

Determine the Questions You Want to Answer

What are you trying to learn or prove? Perhaps you are trying to identify the date and location of a great-grandfather's death. You must evaluate the evidence you've already discovered to determine what you already know. When did your great-grandfather live and where? Do you have any evidence pointing to where he might have died? Do you know his religious affiliation and, if so, do you know the name of the church to which he belonged? If not, do you know the names of all the churches of that denomination in that area at the time?

Do you have any records indicating who his spouse(s) was (were), and when and where they lived, died, and were buried? Could your great-grandfather have been buried with an earlier spouse and her family? Could he have been buried with his parents? Did he have any children and if he did, is it possible that he lived with one of them at the end of his life. Perhaps he was buried with them or in an in-law's family cemetery plot? Did he have siblings and, if so, is it possible that their records might reveal information about his death and burial?

Identify All Potential Resources

It is important to determine what possible resources might provide the information you seek *or* might point you to other materials. You will therefore need to develop a list of as many possible record types that might provide the information.

Remember that you will need to work with both traditional and electronic resources in tandem.

In the third edition of his book *How to Do Everything: Genealogy,* George discusses death records in great detail. He recognized that it is not always possible to locate a death certificate for an individual. In fact, the farther back in time that you research, the less likely it is that official death certificates were issued. He lists fourteen death-related document types, the pieces of information you might expect to find in the document, and the places where you are likely to locate the documents or online records. This list doesn't include funeral home/mortuary records, cemetery interment records, tombstone and cenotaph inscriptions, wills, probate records, estate papers, land records conveying ownership of real property to heirs, dower petitions, guardianship records for any minor children, and any other court records. Any of these might also state the date and place of a person's death.

Obtain Exact Copies of the Original Records

You want to obtain images of the original documents for your personal examination and analysis. These can be photocopies, microform images, photographs, or digitized images of the documents. You may have to order copies of these images, they may be published in a print publication, or they may be accessible in an online database or at an individual's website.

You should also be prepared to produce a source citation for each resource in order to document what it is, where you obtained it, and other pertinent data. (Elizabeth Shown Mills's book *Evidence Explained: Citing History Sources from Artifacts to Cyberspace, Second Edition* [Genealogical Publishing Company, Inc., 2009], describes the accepted standard formats of source citations for more than 1,100 different types of materials.)

Analyze Evidence and Develop Hypotheses

A crime scene investigator gathers all the evidence together and organizes it into some logical arrangement. He or she then proceeds to examine each item to determine what it reveals. This process leads the investigator to develop one or more theories about the problem at hand. Such an analysis often means that the investigator must locate other information in order to clarify or corroborate the meaning of all of the evidence. The investigator frequently needs to repeat the examination process with multiple possible hypotheses in mind.

Your written analysis of each piece of evidence should address the following:

- What is the evidence and how would you describe its physical characteristics and content?

- When and where was the evidence created, how was it produced, who or what entity generated it, and why was it produced?

- Where was the evidence located when you found it, and when did you obtain it? (Was it found in a library or archive, a courthouse or other governmental facility, in personal papers, on the Internet, or received from another researcher?)

- Is the piece of evidence primary or secondary information? Is it an original record (or exact physical image of the original) or a derivative record (a transcript, extract, or abstract, word of mouth, an online family tree, or other non-original material)? In other words, how strong is the source? Do you have a descriptive source citation for the evidence?

- What informational fact does this piece of evidence provide, and how credible is that information? Is there any reason why the information might have been falsified or is otherwise incorrect?

- Does this piece of evidence agree with or corroborate another piece of information found in another source? Is there a conflict with another source? (If so, more research about each source and searches for additional sources are indicated to clarify or resolve any discrepancy.)

Document in detail each hypothesis or scenario in writing. Include a narrative of each theory and describe for each piece of the evidence why you believe it supports your argument.

Include source citations so that you and any subsequent researcher can easily relocate and personally review each item. Even if your work at this time doesn't reach a satisfactory conclusion, you will have documented your analysis in detail so that you can more easily pick up the research trail when you come back to it.

Keep a Research Log

Have you ever visited a library, found a book with information that mentions an ancestor, and photocopied pages, only to find when you returned home that you'd already found the same material and made copies long ago? That is a very common experience. Unfortunately, it also happens when we are doing more extensive—and expensive—research.

Effective genealogical research means not only locating evidence to help prove a fact or a theory but also seeking evidence and finding nothing whatsoever. The lack of documentation can also suggest the absence of an ancestor in a specific area at a particular time. It is therefore important to keep track of what you have researched and what you may— or may not—have found.

A research log is a comprehensive list of the sources you have searched or that you plan to search. It typically includes the name of the source, the purpose of your search, notes about any significant findings, source citations, and notations of what you did not find. You may also record strategies that did or did not work. A well-documented research log focuses your attention on quality research, prompts you to create quality source citations, and helps prevent you from unnecessarily duplicating your efforts.

There are many ways to create and maintain a research log and a number of tools to help. You can start with a to-do list and transfer your findings to a list of completed research for use as a reference. Alternatively, you can use your research log as both a to-do list *and* as a catalog of completed research items.

Your research log can be set up to trace your work for a specific person, a family group, or an entire surname. You might also consider keeping track of a surname in a particular geographic area. Another version of the log could record all the sources you have used, such as all the books you have referred to in tracing a person or a line.

Let's look at some of the options you might consider. You will want to examine several or all of these to determine which one(s) might be best for you. Whatever choice (or choices) you decide to use, a research log will help you focus on the research paths you have taken and concentrate on narrowing your research to new resources.

A Paper Research Log

There will always be people who want to maintain a paper document. You will find that a number of preformatted research log documents are available on the Internet, which you can download and use.

- Ancestry.com has two forms that might be helpful to you. The first is called a Research Calendar (http://www.ancestry.com/trees/charts/researchcal.aspx) and can be used to record "every record source you have searched and serves as a reminder of what you have already done and where you have found pertinent information." The second is the Source Summary (http://www.ancestry.com/trees/charts/sourcesum.aspx). This provides a great way to keep track of all the resources you have consulted in your research on a person or a family. It can save you the time and expense of copying materials or buying books that you have already used. "It is helpful to be able to refer quickly to information you have found for a particular family and the sources of that information. Keep a separate source summary of information found for each family group." Both of these documents are available as PDF files that you can download and print.

- FamilySearch offers its Research Log as both a PDF file (https://familysearch.org/learn/wiki/en/images/5/50/Research_Log.pdf) and as a Microsoft Word document (https://wiki.familysearch.org/en/

images/0/0f/Research_Log.doc). The latter allows you to type in your results. You'll also find an example of a completed research log at http://wiki.familysearch.org/en/images/4/4a/Research_Log_Example.pdf.

Use a Spreadsheet

You can create your own research log using any spreadsheet program. Columns can be defined that include the following type headings:

- **Date** This is the date the research was performed. You'll want to refer to this column in the event that resources, such as websites and new editions of reference books, become available.

- **Repository** Keep track of where you searched, including libraries and archives where one-of-a-kind documents or manuscripts were researched. You also want to record the online websites you have searched, such as Ancestry.com, FamilySearch.org, findmypast.com, Fold3.com, and NewspaperARCHIVE.com. Remember that online sites add new content and update data on a frequent basis, and you will want to check the sites again.

- **Type of Material** Use this column to indicate if the resource is an original document; a printed book, newspaper, or periodical; a transcript, abstract, or extract; microform; an online database; a website; a mailing list or private e-mail; a message board; or another item.

- **Content** Describe what you found, and supply some reference to help identify or distinguish a photocopy, image, or other format of the finding.

- **Analysis** What does this item prove or disprove? Make notes to indicate if the resource provides no information.

- **Link** Provide the URL for the website that was located online and/or a link back to the exact record if possible.

- **Date Accessed** Record the date on which you worked with the item or evidence.

All of this information will be helpful when you are entering data into a genealogy database and when creating an effective source citation. One of the benefits of using a spreadsheet as a research log is that you can later sort the data for further examination. For example, you might sort the spreadsheet by repository so that you can tell what data you located there. This can be helpful when planning a return trip because it will help you avoid duplicating previous work.

A Blog as Research Log

We mentioned earlier in the book that a number of genealogists use a blog as their research log. They record their research experiences, including places they have visited, records they have found, and what their research revealed. They often include images of the original documents and other evidence that they find.

Use Your Genealogy Database Program

Genealogy software programs typically provide an electronic to-do list tool, usually at a person or family level, or at an overall. This allows you to identify specific action items; put your goals in writing; and determine a specific repository, database, or website where you want to perform your research.

RootsMagic provides the capability to create a general research log or one log for an individual or family. You also can create individual to-do tasks for an individual, a family, or in general. The to-do tasks can be transferred to a research log. (You can create a new research log if one does not exist.) You can view your to-do list or research log and can print them to take along on your research trips.

Software Utility Programs

There are three genealogy software programs that can help in locating additional resources, managing the electronic filing of information on your findings, and validating the quality of the resources. These are, respectively, GenSmarts (http://www.gensmarts.com), Clooz (http://www.clooz.com), and Evidentia (http://evidentia.ed4becky.net). You will want to investigate these programs.

The focused analysis of the evidence you have already acquired over time will help you develop a strong research plan to attack your brick wall problems. The use of tracking tools such as a research log and/or blog, and the use of one of the software tools mentioned previously can help in demolishing the research roadblocks. Now, however, is the time to advance your research by using one or more of the techniques we've presented in the book.

The Case of Mary Ann Reilly Smith

While growing up, Drew didn't hear many stories about his Smith ancestors from Newark, New Jersey, but the one story that was repeated from time to time was that the Smiths once had money. What wasn't discussed in any detail was how the Smiths got that money, or where it went, although there was a mention of a Newark-based glass factory.

The first break in the case came from a newspaper story that appeared in the *New York Sun* on 24 March 1897. (See Figure 9-1.) The obituary of Mary Ann Reilly Smith, widow, indicated that, at the time of her death, she was one of the wealthiest women in Newark, and that she had made money from developing the American Glass Bending and Beveling Works. The obituary went on to say that her husband, whose first name was not given, had died in 1872, but no details were provided as to how he died or where he was buried. And the obituary could not have provided details as to what happened to the family fortune after 1897. These questions remained as brick walls at the time of the discovery of the obituary (and similar obituaries in the Newark, New Jersey, newspapers).

A review of family papers provided additional information. After Mary Ann Smith's death, her estate remained undistributed due to her stipulation that the distribution be made directly to her grandchildren upon the death of her last son. However, her next-to-youngest son, Thomas Jefferson Davis Smith, was born in 1865 but did not die until 1958. He was the last of her

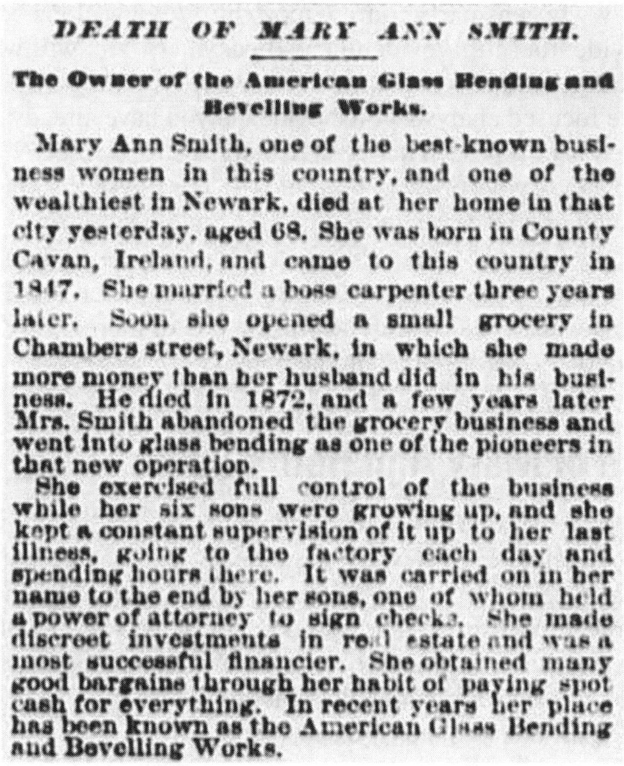

DEATH OF MARY ANN SMITH.

The Owner of the American Glass Bending and Bevelling Works.

Mary Ann Smith, one of the best-known business women in this country, and one of the wealthiest in Newark, died at her home in that city yesterday, aged 68. She was born in County Cavan, Ireland, and came to this country in 1847. She married a boss carpenter three years later. Soon she opened a small grocery in Chambers street, Newark, in which she made more money than her husband did in his business. He died in 1872, and a few years later Mrs. Smith abandoned the grocery business and went into glass bending as one of the pioneers in that new operation.

She exercised full control of the business while her six sons were growing up, and she kept a constant supervision of it up to her last illness, going to the factory each day and spending hours there. It was carried on in her name to the end by her sons, one of whom held a power of attorney to sign checks. She made discreet investments in real estate and was a most successful financier. She obtained many good bargains through her habit of paying spot cash for everything. In recent years her place has been known as the American Glass Bending and Bevelling Works.

FIGURE 9-1 Obituary from the *New York Sun* on 24 March 1897

children to die. This meant that the estate was not settled until more than 60 years after her death. A multi-page document prepared by a law firm provided not only the names and addresses of all surviving grandchildren, but also the fraction of the wealth that each received. (See Figure 9-2.) According to the terms of the distribution, Drew's own grandfather had received 1/144 of the remaining estate, and other legal documents suggested that the estate had not been well managed during the 60 years that the grandchildren waited. This, at least, explained much about where the "Smith fortune" had ended up, and with whom.

What about Mary Ann Smith herself? Drew had heard from family that she was buried with other family members in Holy Sepulchre Cemetery, which sits on the line dividing Newark and East Orange, New Jersey, and since the 1950s had even been underneath part of the Garden State Parkway.

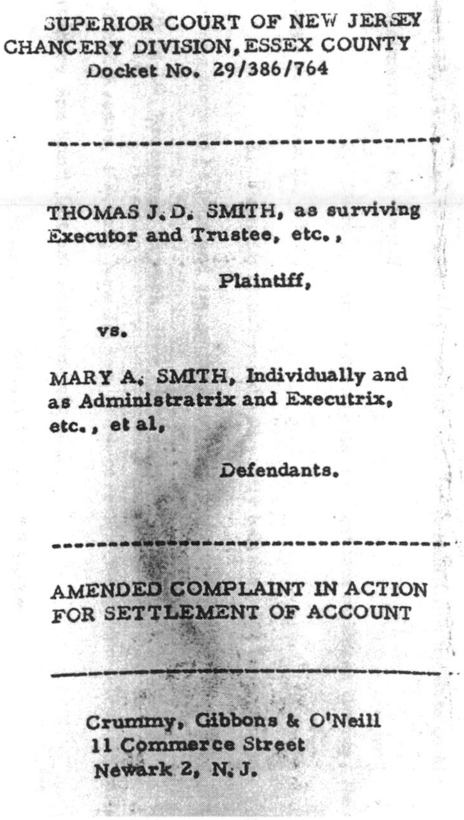

SUPERIOR COURT OF NEW JERSEY
CHANCERY DIVISION, ESSEX COUNTY
Docket No. 29/386/764

THOMAS J. D. SMITH, as surviving
Executor and Trustee, etc.,

Plaintiff,

vs.

MARY A. SMITH, Individually and
as Administratrix and Executrix,
etc., et al,

Defendants.

AMENDED COMPLAINT IN ACTION
FOR SETTLEMENT OF ACCOUNT

Crummy, Gibbons & O'Neill
11 Commerce Street
Newark 2, N. J.

FIGURE 9-2 Jacket cover of legal document regarding Mary Ann Smith's estate

Drew had never been to the burial location of his great-great-grandmother and, living in Florida more than 1,100 miles away, he had no immediate plans to visit the cemetery. However, Drew had mentioned the cemetery on The Genealogy Guys Podcast a number of times, and at least two listeners responded with offers to visit and take photos. One of those listeners did, in fact, locate the grave marker for the Smith family, and e-mailed over 100 digital images to Drew.

It might have been easy to look only at the images that specifically showed Mary Ann Smith's name and ignore the others, but the Good Samaritan had taken photos of each side of the main Smith monument, and on one side were listed the names and death years of Drew's great-grandparents, Charles Henry Smith and Mary Ann Bannon Smith, and below their names, the names of two of their sons, including Drew's own grandfather, William Henry Smith, who had died in 1961.

You can see that paying attention to details and using crowdsourcing were useful in locating details about the life and death of Mary Ann Reilly Smith (and some of her children). But what else could be done with this family, given its common surname? Drew had reason to travel to Salt Lake City, and while there took advantage of the resources of the FamilySearch Library (then the Family History Library) to view microfilmed copies of baptism and marriage records for Newark's St. James Catholic Church. Figure 9-3 shows the FamilySearch Library catalog record for the microfilm containing images from the parish registers of the church. The images on this film were not indexed, which meant that Drew had to adopt the brute force technique of looking at every entry. It appeared that

Parish registers, 1854–1929

Authors: Catholic Church. St. James (Newark, New Jersey) (Main Author)
Format: Manuscript/Manuscript on Film
Language: English
Publication: Salt Lake City, Utah : Filmed by the Genealogical Society of Utah, 1983
Physical: on 3 microfilm reels ; 35 mm.

Notes

Microfilm of originals at McLaughlin Library, Seton Hall University South Orange, New Jersey.

Includes groom index to marriages which are undated.

Some of the records are duplicate copies of parts of the original record.

Subjects

New Jersey, Essex, Newark - Church records

Film Notes

Note	Location	Film/DGS
Baptisms, marriages 1854-1869 Baptisms, marriages 1858-1874 Baptisms 1874-1897 Baptisms 1881-1887	Family History Library US/CAN Film	1378069
Baptisms 1888-1929	Family History Library US/CAN Film	1378070 Items 1-3
Marriages 1868-1918	Family History Library US/CAN Film	1398541

FIGURE 9-3 FamilySearch Library catalog entry for microfilm of the Catholic parish registers of the St. James Church in Newark, New Jersey

there were only two Smith families that were members of that church, one of which was the family of James Smith and Mary Ann Reilly. Drew was able to transcribe the records for their sons and grandchildren.

At this point, most of Drew's questions about his Smith ancestors in the United States were answered, although a few questions remained. What had happened to Mary Ann Reilly Smith's husband, James Smith? When exactly did he die? And how exactly did Mary Ann Reilly Smith end up in the glass-bending business? The answers to these questions would have to wait for a number of years. Between 2006 and 2011, Google had digitized a number of newspapers, and both Drew and his brother, Jeff, took advantage of this to search for information about the Smiths. In early 2012, Drew located an article from the 28 September 1890 issue of the *Newark Sunday Call,* which provided a two-column feature article in the form of a biography of Mary Ann Reilly Smith with an emphasis on her business dealings. (See Figure 9-4.) However, it described in some detail the last days of James Smith, including where he worked, and how he died 17 years earlier.

The article went on to describe how her oldest son, Phillip (identified as "Phil") had become involved in the glass-bending business, and eventually had his own shop, but for unknown reasons had not been able to make a long-term success of it. Because of her honest and reliable reputation, Mary Ann was able to obtain a loan, purchase the business in 1883, and develop it into a huge success. Finally, the article mentioned her companion, a "niece of her dead husband." This description would appear to refer to a woman named in the estate's legal document, Catherine Burke, who is also buried in the Smith plot and whose name and nickname ("Kitty") appear on the side of the same monument previously described.

Are there still unanswered questions? Certainly. Where is James Smith buried? Where in Ireland did he come from? Drew has taken a DNA test that confirms his Irish origins, but does not yet provide enough information to pin down a more exact location. Another newspaper article from the

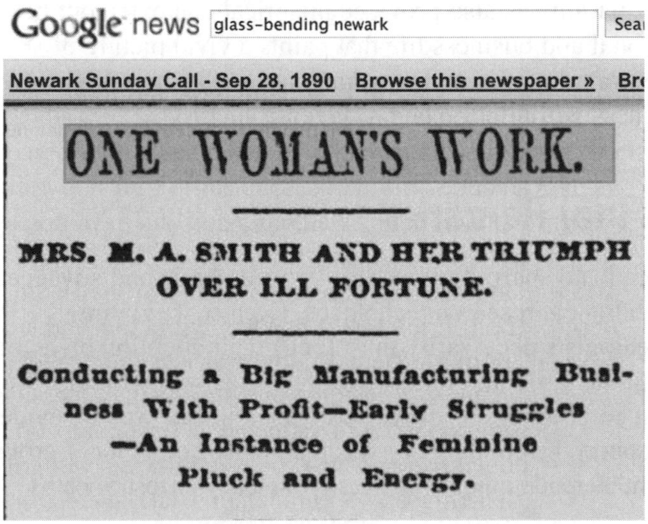

Figure 9-4 Header from the *Newark Sunday Call* of 28 September 1890 concerning Mrs. Mary Ann Smith

Google news   glass-bending newark

Newark Sunday Call - Sep 28, 1890   Browse this newspaper »

ONE WOMAN'S WORK.

MRS. M. A. SMITH AND HER TRIUMPH OVER ILL FORTUNE.

Conducting a Big Manufacturing Business With Profit—Early Struggles —An Instance of Feminine Pluck and Energy.

mid-twentieth century concerns one of Drew's distant cousins and says that James Smith was from a particular Irish county, but that's the only clue so far. It appears to be time to go back through all of the techniques again and see which ones should be applied at this point.

In the meantime, Drew and George have collaborated to locate other resources about Mary Ann Smith and her family. These include:

- Newark city directories that list Mary Ann Smith's residence and those of some of her sons, as well as the business listings for the American Glass Bending and Beveling Works

- Google Maps and its Street View facility to see the surviving buildings of the American Glass Bending and Beveling Works

- Two Digital Sanborn Fire Insurance Maps for Newark from different years that show the glass factory's construction and development, as well as its floor plan, which includes the glass furnaces, work tables, and office spaces

So far, the use of multiple research techniques has enabled Drew to locate a wide array of information and evidence to get past Drew's brick walls with Mary Ann Smith. This information has also provided historical context about her personal and business life that paints a vivid picture of an extraordinary woman making a place for herself in the business world in the late nineteenth century.

Some Final Remarks

There is no sharp dividing line between basic and advanced genealogical research techniques. Even so, beginning genealogists necessarily must focus their attention on learning about the basic and robust research process and on discovering what common kinds of records exist that can provide evidence to support the building of a reliable family tree. A lot of progress might be made quickly and easily on many ancestral paths.

There is no question, however, that persistent genealogists will eventually encounter a brick wall in each of their chosen family lines. In some cases, the paper trail goes back in time only so far and, except for DNA testing, little can be done to push the history further back. In most cases, the path has led to a time or place where existing records seem sparse, confusing, or overwhelming. This is usually where frustration sets in and little or no further progress is made.

This book was written with the genealogist in mind who has already completed the easier parts of research and who wants to move past the frustrations. With experience, a genealogist might discover for themselves many, if not all, of the techniques described in this book. We felt that genealogists would appreciate a more structured approach to attacking brick wall problems, as opposed to a large compendium of brief tips that don't seem to connect to each other in a meaningful way.

If, as the saying goes, it isn't the destination that matters, but the journey, then think of this book as providing you with new ways to conduct that journey, even if you may never reach the destination.

Your best option, at this point, is to take one of your own brick wall problems, review the various techniques in this book, and identify two or three techniques that you haven't tried before but that look promising. When you achieve some success on that problem or on a different one, contact us at The Genealogy Guys Podcast site and let us know. The story of *your* success may serve to inspire numerous other genealogists who otherwise thought that they were permanently stuck. We hope to hear from you!

Index

S